GREAT BALLS OF FLOWERS

BY STEVE ABEE

A Write Bloody Book
Nashville. Los Angeles. USA

WRITE BLOODY PUBLISHING
NASHVILLE, TN

Great Balls of Flowers
by Steve Abee

Write Bloody Publishing ©2009
1ˢᵗ printing.
Printed in NASHVILLE, TN USA

Cover Designed by Nathan Warkentin
Interior Layout by Lea C. Deschenes
Type set in Helvetica Neue and Bell MT
Edited by Derrick Brown, shea M gauer, Saadia Byram and Michael Sarnowski
Proofread by Jennifer Roach

To contact the author, send an email to writebloody@gmail.com

GREAT BALLS OF FLOWERS

THANKS

I dedicate these poems to Cat, Penelope, and Maya because they are the life that I write about. Also, I must thank Ryan Wilson and everyone at the Black Boot. Also, I have to thank David Trinidad for pointing out Ted Berrigan. I must thank my job as a teacher cause that's where I work and also where I get to feel crazy feelings of transcendence and demoralization. It's amazing. I must also thank all the chairs I have sat in to write these things, notebooks, cars that have taken me to work, the beach, wherever. I must thank the food I have eaten and the sun as it rose and set and inspired me in all it's phases. Lastly, I liked to also dedicate these poems to Ralph Abee, my father.

And we are put on earth a little space,
that we may learn to bare the beams of love.

—William Blake

HAIL TO THE THINGS I CANNOT SEE

Hail to thee, oh unseen things. Hail
stellar contraction shaping dust into a sun,
atoms waiting in darkness to begin
their fusion blooming solar fire,
electricity chewing across the wires in the wall,
neuron signal causing the heart to beat,
hormonal impulse causing pubic hair to grow,
synaptic exchange causing the mind to change.
I cannot see any of you, but I know you are there.

Hail
Oh ovum tumbling out of the fallopian waiting room,
into the clean blood darkness, alone,
waiting for brother sperm.
Oh seed generated from testicular emptiness,
looting and rioting in the vaginal night,
I salute all you unseen makers.

Oh heartbeat, accelerated
by smell of a shampoo
that reminds of junior high school French kissing,
first touching vagina, exciting stink, who knew
it would smell like that?

Oh sorrow held in chest cavity
upon the smell of incense

that parents burned to create atmosphere
during their alcoholic stupors, apartments of black outrage
with Charlie Parker's Tunisian horn
blowing holes into the night.

Oh rain of tenderness falling on face,
brought on by memory of candle making
with mother on the porch of the apartment,
colored wax dripped into shapes carved in sand—
Hail to all of you, the invisible evokers of time past
and the things that happened and shouldn't have
and should have, and had to, but what do I know?

Oh wind keeping seagulls aloft, squawking and hovering
over my daughters' and my hot dogs down at Santa
     Monica Pier.

Oh gravity that holds the trees up and my bones together,
web of sun's stellar radiance that wraps this earth,
sphere of mud and bones, in perfect location
for the growing of our brains and other cosmic windows.

Oh sunlight, tinkerer of soul and mind,
creating my waking and seeing with your clear yellow light,
waking me with your rising, pulling me to sleep when you go,
my body like the oceans in their tides.
I am you, all of me, I believe.

Oh sorrow, endless holes in the sky and in the heart,
you are there again, purple thing, river-like, deliverer,

brokenly smiling the way to light.

Oh silence, kindest hush of mind and time,
loving terminus of all, the sky of purest now.
Silence, holding and blooming sounds
of airplanes passing through clouds,7th graders
whispering in the back row, heart beats
like bubbles coming to the surface of the water,
all rising from silence, all stone and gaseous
vapor and vision laying upon silence.
Love laying upon the silence, sunrise
out of silence.

Oh Hail, hail
invisible things.

I LOVE THE SUNSHINE

It's 6:30 a.m.

I'm in love with the sunshine,
the sun that shines all night.

I don't want no foreign chemicals in my body.
There is only sorrow and no love in that.
My sorrow must have love.

What do I see here? The sky is blue
in my mind. My neighbors start their cars.
Garbage trucks sigh, and squawk
and hum lifting garbage up
and tossing it into their big mouths.
They are loud and smell but are symbolic, personal
for I, too, am a big mouthed garbage truck
clattering lyric dirt and stink
through the neighborhoods of dawn and I am

recalling life as a young kid in Santa Monica
watching garbage trucks slip their forks
into the side slots of the metal apartment bins
and lift and flip all the egg shell cigarette cat litter
into the hydraulic guts and belly. It was
sexual. I can see that now.

Santa Monica trash trucks were sky blue
and filthy.

It's 6:42 and
you can't see what I feel, anywhere.
But I feel it everywhere.

Ted Berrigan roamed New York
while his babies slept.

And I sleep in the room next to my pretty ones
and wake to work for all our loves
and Ted Berrigan roams
through the city my heart has
built of poetry.
Oh Baudelaire, you don't have to
do anything here.
It's all done.

The sky turns its blue all the way up.
It's simple.

God Bless Pepsi-Cola, donuts,
sun.

ECHO PARK POOL

I'm at the Echo Park Indoor Swimming Pool,
thinking about sonnets, watching my daughter, Penelope, swim.
She's learning how to do the free style.
She lifts her arm up out of the water. Then the other one. She lifts
her head out of the water to breathe. She stops and stands
    and starts
again. It's a lot to do.

There are a bunch of kids splashing in the pool all around her.
She swims around them.
A woman in blue swims in the deep part of the pool.
She comes to the wall, flips around, and glides the other way.
The life guard is a cute girl, small, with dark hair, and soft smile.

The pool is blue. The water looks blue
but I know it is not. It is water, clear and the color
of your hand.

My daughter makes fun of other kids.
What can I say.
I am sitting on cement steps, looking at the pool
and I am sad because I am reading poetry
and that's what poetry does to me and I like it.

Poetry is all about having people talk about you
when you're not there.

Penelope, Penelope—
the name is like jewels and balloons to me.
Maya, her little sister, is like the ocean, glassy waves rolling
in to shore like the back of a whale
and she is like that to me.

A little girl runs up to her mom,
asks her to fix something on her suit.
She's got that look on her face, where you
can tell what she'll look like when she's a teenager,
but right now she doesn't know how to fix her suit
and she needs help so she's got that I-need-help look,
the I-don't-know-how-to-do-this look and it's okay,
I was always freaked out to need help.
It's a great look, very wise, very open.

The thing is we need each other,
but I suspect people of plotting to destroy me with
their help. I realize this is a problem.

I think of holding my wife in bed, spoons, I feel golden,
like gold is shining through me. I am golden at the
       swimming pool.

So Penelope is learning to swim
and it strikes me that God must be
like a bunch of parents sitting there,
watching their kids learn to swim,
letting them learn, looking up from their conversations

or books to see if everything is cool,
walking over to the side of the pool if there is a problem,
but mostly letting the life-guard deal with it,
and the kids splash around,
float, get freaked, stand up, float again.

GAS

I.
Steve Abee is a gas station.
The Lord Jesus Christ is a gas station.
Jack Fris is a gas station.
Jack Kerouac is a gas station, too.
We are all gas stations, lonesome lovely gas stations
on the sandy skirt edge of the desert
dispensing starlight octane to each other as we move
from seashore to graveyard.

Time blows its bony nose into a Dixie cup
in the back of a Tijuana Greyhound.

The rain on the street smells like wet feathers.
The sky looks like a bowl of gray marbles.
The cloud kisses the rooftops.
Police cars, fire trucks, air raid horns, ambulances
wail sirens across the sky like John Coltrane
in cacophonic meditation on love and suffering.
I taste the rain that falls from that horn.
It tastes blue.

That 3 am the boy drove his car into the wall,
I could feel his breath dripping down the sidewalk
back to the sea.

Catherine Uribe is my wife. She speaks God.
Jerusalem, Jerusalem whisper the doorways.

II.
I am not a gas station. I have no fuel for you.
I am a mini mart. I fill the pre-dawn
nacho sauce need of the unwashed
and addicted.

The earth is in line for some meteoric hand jive.

When I lick your secrets the bombs begin to fall from your thighs.
It isn't polite to scream *fuckin' dick shit* in the middle of the
    night when
the whole house is asleep.

The shimmering tongue of disaster licks our wounds
like a child licking the sugar dust from a Pixie Stick.
It is not the fire spilling from the windows
that causes me to be full of fear and dread,
but the trees who watch from the street
not understanding the orange tendrils of hatred and power.
It is not the sky that signifies endlessness
but your fingers pointing to the silence
that surrounds what you just said.

I turn into a plastic army man,
get lost in the backyard
and live on the nectar of the weeds.

III.
The Vexer responds with incredulity at being told how to
      write a poem.
The Vexer mocks the sounds of happiness that come from his belly.
His children tickle him on the green carpet. He cracks
up, turns to dust.

IV.
The world will create a toilet that knows what it is doing.
The world will stop at the stop lights and go at the go lights.
The world will stop fighting gravity, will accept
the truth of its own light.
The world will learn to whistle.
Our Gargantuan psychic underwear will be cleaned.
The time bomb within, full of high octane denial
will finally burst when all is created again.
Vamanos ala chingada.

Late at night the goldfish turns the light on in its aquarium,
sits on the rock, troubled by the mystery of water.
John Coltrane steps from his limousine at the Last Chance Gas.
The sun sets, he nods to the music in his hands.
Good-bye, Good-bye cry the golden horns of Jerusalem.

ARS POETICA

The kid walks in
to the Jack in the Box
with his little brother.

There's a bum, a mute, who stinks
like trash and wine. He's drinking
coffee from a stained cup.

His coat bulges
with scraps of paper,
coupons and match books.

The kids know him.
He calls them over
and writes on the back

of a card he pulls
from his pocket,
an advertisement

for old coins.
The kid and his brother
look at the card, the coins ,

the words. The old man
stares at them, the need
to be understood

hanging from his face
like a stone. The kid can't read.
He's only in first grade.

The man smiles and points
to the counter. The kid takes
the note to the woman

working there, his brother
watching everything. She
reads it, and pours

a new cup of coffee
for the old guy.

NEW CHAIR POEM

Sometimes I feel so bad it hurts to look at anything.
Sometimes I feel so good it hurts but in a different way.
I'm sitting in a black chair that I got today at St. Vincent De Paul.
I'm looking out on the roofs of El Sereno.
I want this to be a poem. I want this to be pure word.
What is pure word? Hard to say, but that's what I mean
when I say poem? The thing is when I say poem,
I'm really thinking of lights, lights that open you.
singing open all night. A girl
named Heather said my words were like the Aurora Borealis,
How'd I do that? I don't think I did that. Something else did that.
Something else does all of this, the roofs, the day, clouds,
children, my children, this house, our house, the bank does that,
but the whole house, the big house that everything is,
that I am, who does that? The I house, who does that?
Now I'm feeling green broken things with wings floating
     in the sky inside.
It's nice. It's sad. Can you dig it? Can you dig it all?
This is the question the earth asks me, everyday.
It's a lesson, you know, sitting down, digging.
It is personal, just you and a rock and some bugs.
My daughter in the next room, watching TV,
comes into the room where I'm at,
says she wants to write this poem with me.
It's like that. Personal. It's hard. You get mad.
Oh what these children of mine have done to me?

They took everything.
Do you know how hard that was for me? One who spent so
much time inside my stuff, pleasing myself and myself only.
I got nothing left and now I'm happy, can you dig that?
A woman said my life was small.
I said "It ain't small.
It's safe." That is, I'm not killing myself faster than
life is and I'm not missing what the God of Time is
giving to me, whisper sauce, good night sauce,
love life sauce, yes, I'm seeing this.
Yes, Penelope you can make this book with me.
Yes, my 9-year-old daughter, freckled teacher, maker of me,
yes, you can make this book with me.
You already have.

I AM TIRED OF PEEING

I am tired of peeing.
How long is this supposed
to go on?
Why all the waste, all the time?
What does it mean?
Ernest Hemmingway counted his craps
then killed himself.
Did he realize that we
aren't really here?

TO THE SAD PEOPLE

You want to
fly across it all,
be swift over the roof tops.
Oh wingless thing,
just sit and
let it have you.
Let it have you.
Let it all have you
and lift you.

LOVE POEM

I long for the spill and sea
of soft kiss touch her holy now.

Oh sing, you goddamn spheres.

She explodes
all over me
and I into her
and we are both
late to work.

MONKEY KING SINGS
(FOR KIRK PODELL)

The darkness has seeped into the water supply,
the Monkey Kings are losing
the ecstatic battle.

I am here with my
conflict daffodils, sperm cup anarchy,
yes, right here with my soft drink angels,
the compassionate disease all around.
The armies of neglect are at the castle walls, but they
     don't even see me,
and the schizophrenic rain
is trying to speak false sugar to my lonely nest.
It isn't fair to the statues, but I have
stolen their silence and hold it in my hands
like sunlight.

Oh cascade of womb, oh fallopian parade,
it is time to separate the milk
from the eggs.
Oh curse the sailors, but love the men of benevolent impulse,
fill this tattered soda can with oceans of fire and gold .

I swim through all the milk-man stars
and open like a flower between the cars.

PENELOPE AND ME POEM #35

Does the grass bloom flowers?
The sidewalk does because it feels like it.
The sidewalks bleed the color of your shoe, not mine.
I want to hold your skies.
I want to breathe your secret things.
You can't be serious. There's nothing
I won't do for you. But, man, you ask
a lot. So what, I can ask anything.
    I'm the wonderer.
I wonder…does love grow on trees?
Can stress go too far?
Can that feeling in your belly kill you?
What about the love that makes your arms stretch
like trees through the orange street light?
Does the sidewalk bloom? Yes.
It bloomed you. It bloomed you.

THIS POEM HAS A MIND OF ITS OWN

This poem has nothing to say.
It is a mute poem, afflicted at birth.
It just sits and watches you
as you try to stick the refrigerator plug into the wall
but can't because there isn't enough room
to maneuver your fingers, and
this poem won't get up to help you as you start to get
    more upset cause
you can't get the damn plug into wall, and you think of all
the other shit that won't fit. This poem just stares at you.
This poem won't even get up to get out of your way.

You want to throw something at this poem.
You don't like this poem because this poem doesn't like you,
it'll spit on you and you know it.
It's fed up with your emptiness,
with your hole-in-my-heart reality,
and all the rest of your personal wound as alphabet bullshit

This poem knows where you keep the titty mags, videos,
the weed, why your kids
don't want to play with you,
knows that you got so many chemicals
inside of you
you're just afraid your heart will burst
on you at any moment.

This poem knows why you can't be with anyone
for too long.

This poem does not respect you.
This poem is making fun of you.
Fuck this poem!
Throw it against the wall.
Watch as it falls crying, and crawls out the door.
You think about following it
out to the sidewalk and killing it.
You're so insane you want to bash the fucker's
head into the cement.
Yeah, then it would be better.
Then everything would be better.

MAYA'S POEM

It's almost noon. I'm feeling soft today. No edges. This is my second poem and my third cup of tea. There are cherries on the table, bananas, some freckled which means they are soft and banana bread is soon.

My wife is in the next room talking to the Holy Spirit.

She does that all the time now. It is very inspiring and very impressive. My grandmother came to her. I cried. Still, we can't afford to buy a house. That is not too inspiring. So I'm thinking about God and house. I look at Lucille's house next door. It is a very nice house and then I think about God like a house, then life like a house, a house made of God, and then I look at my house, green walls, red walls, and I think about spiritual paths, which way, what to do, and everything says "Be still and listen, that's all." So I listen, get soft, look at the bananas, begin to write this poem.

I drink some more tea. I read another poem by Ted Berrigan. It's about all these things he won't do again and I start looking at my poem, my tea. I think: I won't drink this tea again. I won't read this poem again. Everything changes. I'll do it again, but it won't be the same, and neither will I and that makes me a little sad.

I look outside. It's a beautiful day. I mean it is a beautiful day, really, profoundly. It's got warm sunlight, a blue sky, a breeze, shadows, shade, saws buzzing, wheels rushing by, buses, Junior looking for Larry my neighbor, birds and more birds singing layers upon layers of birdsong. The songs move across the roof of my mind, infinite, yes, but small and fragile, a song moving miles away, until finally it disappears into the whole sky.

My youngest daughter, Maya, walks into the hallway. She's four years old, not in school, today. She looks at me as she goes into the bathroom, smiles lovely rascal smile, dressed only in chonies; she goes to the bathroom, talks to herself, but not just herself, not really, more like all of us, the way kids do because self isn't set so much. "Is lunch ready?" she asks in her small stuttering song voice, as she comes out. Her voice opens me like breath.

What's the difference now?
I'm trying to be good now.
I'm not trying to be bad.
I mean, I care. That's the difference.

Car horns, car alarms, Holy Spirit, birds, a shovel, cigarette smoke (smell) voices of smokers, skill saws, a can of tuna being opened.

THINGS TO DO

Clean my desk.

Look out the window forever.

Wait for the robin to bring the pomegranate seed of eternal
spring and sex to my backyard
and watch it grow and grow.

Get up in the morning and brush my hair. Just brush my hair.

Get up in the morning and then go back to sleep, pull her
    close to me,
fall down into the warm sea of her breath. It's true,
it is that deep.

Buy an engine from the machine shop of night.
Order one starry dynamo,
and a bag of heavenly connection.
Tip the Angel Headed Hipster.

Learn how to repair my own Angelic car.

Listen to the radio, any station, and weep at the miracle of
    language,
drink my tea, and agree with it all.

Buy an alarm clock that wakes me up
and puts on my clothes, and gives me plenty of time
to meditate and write.

Turn the water of the mind off
before it floods everything
and comes through the window
and ruins the couch of complacency
on which I nap.

Oh, let the water wake me. Be not afraid of your own mind's water.

Quit writing, stop forever, lie down on the floor,
make amends for all the bad words and wrong words I
    have ever written,
burn something, weep, apologize to the dawn sky
because you have misused it so.

Take another nap.

Develop a healthy form of coma.

Learn to levitate over things that aren't there.

Make a drip castle on the sea shore of melancholia.

Fail the test of time.

Then create my own test,
but forget to study, fail it, then kick myself out of

my own school.

Not create anything to last.

Bring the trumpet of my sorrow to my lips, play it loud
and bad, out the window of my 1942 Hope Street
apartment, sending that note through the fire-escapes,
down the curbs, through the car light, street light,
through the light in the bones of the man drinking a
cup of coffee at Jim's Café, looking out the window,
looking back at his hand, checking the clock on the
wall, thinking it's time and then laughing to himself,
"Time for what?" Ah yes, the trumpet I will play.

Invent a math that I am expert in, that I know all the
answers to, that I can use in my own personal sciences,
measuring the arc of light that comes from my eyes
and lands on your body and causes you to recline
illuminated and awesome on the throne of my mind.
That will be a good math.

Kiss myself good-bye as I go to work.

Change the way I feel about emptiness.

Remember what I was going to say.

Say strange and beautiful things to anyone, especially
when they aren't listening.

Drop this class of time.

Apologize to the lady on the bus who I insulted last week,
    if I happen to see her again and I happen to feel like
    doing it, if I don't get defensive and chicken out.

Paint my mind golden.

Find some paint that doesn't peel off the mind.

Have fun, have lots and lots of fun, have the kind of fun
    that incites riots of envy and panics of desperation.
    Have so much fun that I get shot down like a balloon.

Be a Love Terrorist. Send love bombs in the mail, put love
    in cars, buses, in empty bottles of Sprite left behind
    Jon's market on Vermont. Blow up everyone I see with
    a love bomb. *Ka-Boom!* There, you're loved.

Talk positive to myself. Tell myself it's all okay.
Convince myself that everything is fine.

Wait until tomorrow to really get started.
Begin when I finally get an idea.
Jump in when I find the confidence.

Execute some bad habits. Devise new ways of abolishing
    my hating and resentful mind to the backseat of the
    car that is me and drive myself into the timeless ocean
    of awareness that surrounds every molecular atomic

breath of this very big now of universal bus ride love.

Think of old beatnik cafes in Venice and how lonely and
faraway they must have been,on the slum ocean edge
of 1940's, 50's Los Angeles, a city that barely even
existed. living in the land of oblivion, high in the early
morning low clouds shrouding the Lincoln Boulevard
gas station, dirt lot sand lot next to that, Stuart
Perkhoff writes Art is God is Love on the wall, which
Wallace Berman said, and nobody is watching. But of
course the god of obscurity is watching and that's how
I am thinking of it.

Open the doors of love. Take the door off the entrance
of love. Love must have no door. It must be open. All
the time and for all, but oh that is a scary and strange
door to keep open when some asshole mafia type in
Glendale driving 80 miles an hour almost kills you and
your wife.

Oh, for this I must take down the walls of love. Let love
out of the room.

Realize finally that it was out of the room all along.

Witness the energy of a second grade sock ball game with
my daughter as the sun goes down and an airplane
flies by, and the smog and dust and city junk is lit the
tender pink of life and death.

POEM TO MY WIFE

If I was going to write a poem to you, my love, I would say
   something like:
I love you so much that when I touch you
my fingers turn into miniature suns shining
light across all the most remote Alaskan stellar zip codes of soul.

Yes, and then I would talk about how loving you is like surfing
the universal wave of benevolent impulse, hang ten on
   the wave of benevolent impulse, impulse to explode
   benevolence all over.

If I were to write you a poem, I would use words like hark
   and herald, harmonious, harmonize, hark the herald
   of your harmonious harmonized form, something like
   that.

I would have senseless passages talking about intra-
   heartbeat transit, I would recite cosmo-angelic trolley
   timetables to the innocent seashore of our kiss where
   hippies play tambourine brain-fried ukulele and we
   dance on the crab grass sand.

If I was going to write you a poem, it would have words
   that no one could pronounce, including me. It would
   have unpronounceable words of love. I would use them
   to say everything I am feeling. I would use words

not even said, ever, not even thought of words, words
that when they are even attempted burn the speaker
right up, into a shining ball of Christmas lights, poof,
Holiday flame of love, hot, bright, gone. I would have
some serious unsayable words in my poem.

To be honest, the poem I write would have to have a dark
side, irrational, saying crazy things, unhealthy things,
deeply unreasonable things, things like—I love you too
much to breathe. I love you too much to see. I can't see
because I love you. The poem would say I won't share
you with sunlight, no, sunlight can't even see you,
can't hold you, I won't allow it. No, only I can hold
you and when I can't hold you, then we will have some
problems.

I would say that I cannot share you with time. The clock
gets nothing. I love you before time and after time,
so fuck time. You're mine, not time's. Then the poem
would continue and say I love you too much to share
you with God. I won't share you with God. Though it
was God that made us, brought us together and is us,
simply, breathing and seeing, but fuck that guy, you're
mine now and I won't share.

The poem would be like that, yes, possessive,
uncomfortable, embarrassing, a mistake perhaps, but it
wouldn't be able to help itself, it would be stuck out in
the rain with no place to go except to you.

LOOKING AT THE CURTAINS POEM

It is 8:20 in the evening. August 4th.
I mean, here I am, nowhere else, looking at the curtain
    before me, which is off-white.
My wife put it up. She thought I should be tired of the rag I had
hanging from my window before. She was right. She is
    always right.
I surrender to her pure rightness. It is kind, her pure
    rightness. It is
so kind that it is frightening and offensive to the impure heart.

Have you ever been with pure rightness? I feel it condemning
    me. Pointing a finger at me. Compelling me from my
    darkness, calling attention to it, making me see it,
    know it, forcing me to make a decision. But it's not
    doing anything hurtful on purpose, in fact it is not
    doing anything at all. I am doing all of this while she
    just sits there and says "You need new curtains."

Oh, massage my inner hoopla, pure light of my pure right
    love. She's got a Guru. He came to her in the shower.
    His body died thirty years ago, but that doesn't mean
    beans in Guru land. He loves her. That makes two of
    us. We are the same that way, me and this Guru.

At first I was a little freaked out, guru man in the shower,
    she loves him, he loves her, but really I can't see any

of this anyway and then I thought about it, or really, right now I am thinking about it and it's cool, me and the Guru who is God agreeing like we do about Cathy. I just got to remember this next time I start freaking out.

A bus rolls by. A dog barks. The big Eucalyptus in the backyard hangs like a big shaggy head, all tall and dark and gangling over the swing set. I write this. Penelope reads A Little House in the Big Woods, lying on the green carpet. Maya comes in the room and asks me for a couple of Jo Jo's, which are Trader Joe's oreo cookies. Healthy, though they don't taste like it. I guess it is just a healthier kind of crap.

There is no point here. No point at all, but I can feel it coming, I swear I can, like the sharp tip of the minute hand creeping around the nine, looking for twelve to call it all off and start it up again. Oh, now I'm singing. I love to sing. Every time I sit down to do this I start singing.

The computer corrects me so often, it is getting harder and harder to ignore. It is just being kind, all corrections are kind. All corrections are the hands of love. God is a correction.

The lights are on in the gas station across the street. It's called Magic Gas. I always think of Oklahoma when I look at them. I have never been to Oklahoma, but I

look at the gas station's awnings with the fluorescent
light underneath it and I think of the Outsiders, the
book, which took place in Oklahoma, and it has a scene
with Dally in the phone booth, in the light, raising
his suicidal gun toward the cops. Some little kids ride
bikes in cut-off pants under the light.

Penelope's reading and now eating cookies. My Lord, first
grade and she looks like a fully contained hanging-
out-in-herself-human being, one of us, one of us. We
accept her. What can I say about all of this? Her hair
hanging down on her book. Her voice tripping up and
down the words, pureness, somehow, I don't know how,
but pure, here. The gas station's lights turn off. The
neighborhood kids are still riding around. Can't see
them, but I can hear them, yelling, shrill, laugh, sound
like birds. Penelope reads some more, yawns, closes the
book.

When does this become a poem, I want to know? The
Dodgers are on the TV in the next room. The game is
tied. Now Penelope wants me to play a game with her
in the living room. Who says "no" to that?

When wasn't this a poem? When is any of it not a poem?

TOMORROW I AM 38—PERSONAL POEM #19

Tomorrow I am 38.
37 was good, but it is gone.
Gone is a very true kind of place.
Here is even more true.
Gone is so big and here so small.

Family is out, doing something.
It is nighttime. It is raining.
I didn't go see a movie.
I'm about to turn on the TV
and see if the UCLA basketball game
is on. It's on somewhere.
Sports Center is always on.

I want everything I do to be a poem.
I mean, I sit around thinking things,
watching rain on electrical wires,
clouds in the sky,
dishes in the sink, thoughts about
god, great things, the lottery,
want to write a book,
and I say that'd be a good poem.

So here I am,
another time around the sun,
and it is good this time,

being depressed in an empty house at night
is good, like a river, a street,
always moving, aching
with the love of always wanting
to be full, be empty, empty, be full.

So here I am, on the couch,
Rosie the cat right next to me,
Can of Trick Nuts by the T.V.
Rain, rain everywhere.
Six months from now
the hills will burn, but
Now it's 7:44 p.m. in El Sereno and wet
and all poems should be
this easy, in a bathrobe,
searching for a last line,
to end something that has none.

THANK YOU POEM #2

On behalf of myself and my daughters Penelope
and Maya, I just want to say thank you to whoever was
responsible for the ducks in Echo Park lake last night,
around eight o'clock with the late-day, summer sun light
bouncing off of their speckled feather necks, and the big
bump on the bill of the big honker duck, who ate the fried
Dorito wheels right out of my hand and Penelope's hand,
whose bill nibbled my finger even, but did not hurt,

And also thanks for the fountain spraying white
geysers of water so high into the sky, blue sky, orange sun
mumbling like an old man on a bus to no one, to everyone,

And thanks for the lotus flowers, blooming pink and
white, like breasts, petals like sheets of a gown coming
undone,

And thank you for the play ground and all the other
children, the Mexican kids, the Chinese kids, we all belong
here, we have always belonged here.

And thanks for the Dodgers and Eric Gagne, and for
the ninth inning that looked good, then bad, and good
again and ended that way, Dodgers win 6 to 5, and for the
car radio where I got to listen to that last inning of the
game,

And for my daughters Penelope and Maya, I want

45

to say thank you, thank you for their eyes and hair, and running smiling little kid bodies, running up the slide and sliding down the slide, and running through the grass, and under the trees, to get a raspado from the raspado man.

I must say thanks for the atoms of the air, the molecules conspiring to energize this experience of grass and tree and duck and sun.

ON THE PURCHASING OF LIFE INSURANCE

Well, it is official, I accept that one day I am going to die.

I am going to decay and rot in the ground,
this body will finally fail.

> Oh, I have dared it many times.
> Laughing at its vulnerability as I filled it with chemicals,
> amphetamine rooftop crazed for days thinking
> "I'm gonna become the sunrise and never die."
> I don't do that anymore.

Oh Lord! I'm feeling so ridiculous, so human, is this what
    you meant
when you said "Let there be Light"?

Skin will sag. Muscles will fall.
The paint on the roof of the mind will come off
one green flake at a time.

Who knows what else? Some strand of brain
will probably sputter and fry itself inoperable
and the body will go catatonic while eating green beans.
What if it's like a car running out of gas,
or a ball point pen with just a little ink left?
The hand stops, then starts. The eyes go on, then off.
My children will slap me on the back like a television,
while their children laugh.

Yes!
        I'm going to plop on the ground
        like the piece of walking fruit that I am
        and I, for one, am going to be sad
        to see this body go, cause I like
        this living thing. It has been kind to me,
        as kind as it can be, I think.
        I'm going to die, the end,
        Steve Abee no more,
        gone Daddy, Grandaddy,
        gone words of Pluto Love Sauce,
        gone golden word pudding,
        gone words of starry womanhood and
        manly sorrow magic words, gone
        gone words, all these words,
        and the arms to hold them,
        and this mouth to shape them.

   I am going to die.
Burn the body and read the mind.
I'll be done, and then what?
        Do what I have to do,
        go where I have to go,
        do what must be done?

My deathbed advice to myself: Don't argue.

So the Armenian man
        takes my blood and
        I pee in a cup and he
        puts it all in a tube,
        all to see if I'm healthy enough
        for the insurance company to bet on.

I sign the paper
and feel closer to this world and my body.

    Of course, I am here, for a while I think, but who
    knows, which is why I'm doing all of this, leave my
    family something, all of that and you know, what if the
    psychic is wrong? He said I was going to be rich and
    that hasn't happened.

    But I'm here. More than I was before I signed the paper.
    I'm crazy like that, making ceremonies out of
        everything:
    The crumbs on the kitchen floor are sacred,
    the ring of milk from the cereal bowl,
    lightly apparent on the table, suggests the divine.

    Steve Abee is getting Term Life, twenty-five bucks a month.
    Steve Abee is getting Term Life, twenty-five bucks a month,
    and about the same for the wife.

THE SHAMAN

The Shaman has a job.
The Shaman gets up in the dark to go to work.
Makes a cup of coffee, brushes his teeth, starts the car.
He's late, again. The window is fogged.
The Shaman curses
in traffic. The Shaman wants to know what the hell
Is going on with all the slow cars.
Who is driving?
What is the problem?

The Shaman runs over pigeons
on the way to work.
Thud. Thud. He is sorry.

The Shaman gets to work.
He is a teacher. He teaches kids.
The kids are screaming and yelling.
They love him but they do not listen.
The Shaman laughs to himself,
"Just like me and God."

LETTER TO MY WIFE PRETENDING I HAVEN'T SEEN HER IN YEARS AND THAT I AM NOAH AND LIVING IN LOS ANGELES

Dear Wife,

Here the weather is hot, the air polluted and the fog was thick this morning.

So thick I thought of you. I couldn't see across the little valley where we live, lived

and I thought of you because I couldn't see. I thought of you in there and I was lost and I was late. You could have seen through it all, like you always did, and told me it was time to leave for work, but as it was I was mesmerized in the wet low clouds of dawn and couldn't tell the time.

It all looks the same in the fog.
I got hell from the boss.

Where are you? The children? The animals? The ark that we came here in? No one remembers that. No one remembers that we weren't always here, on the dirt, that we lived on creaking timbers, on waters that would not end.

I'm not writing this to you to make you feel guilty. It's just coming out of me this way. I feel disconnected. Not part of anything. Why? What happened? I was supposed to be the second Adam. I carried the animals. I listened. Now, there's nothing to listen to. When did that happen?

The fog burned off and it got hot. The air conditioning doesn't work. When was the sky anything but burnt? I was looking at the pigeons this morning as I walked to the bus. They always return home, pigeons do. How long have they been there? Were they there before the walls, the bricks, the flood? I don't remember packing them.

And why there, above the corner market? Why is that home? Forever on the roof of the Del Mor Apartments.

I miss you. I feel you in the heat, on my back, walking home from the bus stop.

When are you coming back? When will you be with me? I still smell you in our bed, and taste you in my finger tips. All the time I thought I was looking for something, dry land, new worlds, and all the time it was you. I see that now.

I AM IN LOVE

I am in love.
I waste a lot of time
And I am very busy.
The train is yellow, Union Pacific,
Down the hill, it blows its horn, 3 a.m.
But it is not 3 a.m., not now. Now
it is 6:20 p.m. and I am sleepy.
Gonna take a snooze, then go roller skating.
(Let me tell you about roller skating. It is great.)
Cathy plants plants and Ted Berrigan is great.
His kids are great.
My kids are great.
I have two friends,
Jack and Michael.
And two more, now that I think of it:
Brandon and Kmo,
But nothing daily.
My kids have friends.
I have kids and a wife.
Who needs friends?
I am in love.
Everyone is my friend.
If there is time,
I'll call you.
Harry L.
His girl's a flirt. I like flirts.

They make you feel special even if you ain't.
They just want you to like them, so I do.
Chris Figler. Blake. Now, grey haired
But young, he was a jacker of hearts
And credit cards (once) escaped apprehension
at Vinyl Fetish on Melrose in 1980, something. Remember
    that place?

Time is old. Time is beat. All time is beat time.

Things change. Nothing lasts long enough. That's the point.
It's about the green cypress and the black asphalt
and the jug of Drano Gel in the garage, that's the point.
Why? Why is that? I don't know.

I have two friends. My wife, she plants yaro and sage.
I will plant the sunflowers. Take a nap. Write a poem. A book.
Take a nap. Make friends. Have tea. Go roller skate.

You can't blame me for anything.

IT IS SPRING NOW, MY LOVE

It is Spring now, my love
and I am feeling bent up
and sideways with desire.

It is Spring now, my love
and I want you every day.
I want the dove of your belly.
I want the nest of your sea.
I want the flower of your mind.

It is Spring and
I want the heralds of your form.
I want the headlines of your time.
I want the soft lamp of your kisses
beneath the world.
I want the tender,
not closed, vulnerable sunshine,
of you.

It is Spring now,
and I want to be with you in all the Right Nows that I can have.
I want us around this moon-shaped wound
that unfolds itself every night, disappearing
into the oceans of my brain.
I want your shining things, your light in all things,
the bright shower of your hands

shaping us a New Year's parade, New Year's for everyone
we meet, New Year's all around. Here have a year,
it's on me, us, because it is Spring.

It is Spring, my love, and there are a dozen suns in the refrigerator.
It is Spring, my love, and the light is undeniable.

It is Spring, my love, and I want and I don't know.
It is love, my Spring, and this want is all I know.
It is Spring. It is Love and it is you.
I know this and there is no "don't."

ABOUT LOVE AND LOOKING AT YOU

It is so good to be still
and be able to finally see
you, reclining there, reading a magazine,
face like a moon, nodding at the waves
crossing beneath the carpet of our house;
beautiful, yes, but more than that.
Thank God, I stopped
and you waited for me.

6:15 A.M. PANTOUM

My oldest girl Penelope sleeps like warm bread.
The world of birds sings loud for no reason, except the sun.
I sit quiet drinking my tea, reading my book.
Cathy is sleeping. Maya's sleeping too.

The world of birds sings loud for no reason, except the sun.
I look around the kitchen. I don't know anything.
Cathy is sleeping. Maya's sleeping too.
The sky takes off the night.

I look around the kitchen. I don't know anything.
Cars rush by, the engines of despair.
The sky takes off the night.
On the sun it is always time for lunch.

The cars rush by, the engines of despair.
My girls sleep, all covered in dreams and messed hair.
On the sun it is always time for lunch.
Maya, the youngest, likes to play Clue.

My girls sleep all covered in dreams and messed hair.
They breathe the night out of the sky.
At night, Maya stays up just to play Clue.
She likes to guess the killer.

My girls breathe the night out of the sky.
They think it and then there's the sun.
Maya likes to guess the killer.
Who did it? What room? With what? To whom?

They think it and then, there it is: the sun.
They breathe me. I breathe them. It's love.
Who did it? What room? With what? To whom?
The night comes undone.

SOME RULES

Don't move
when you watch the sunrise.
Sleep all day when the moon
is bright in your dreams.
Miss work if necessary,
but be sure to show your family
bright dream moon
in your mind.
Last thing—
Become as big as the ocean
when you kiss your kids
goodnight,
They will feel safe.

THE GREEN CARPET AND BLUE SKY
OF MY MIND

The carpet is green. The sky is blue and the sun is hot.
I'm not in the sun. I'm in my office typing and watching
the pepper tree nod

in the wind. The red-berried bunches of pepper balls
are right there,

nodding, doing nothing, nothing special,

which is the secret of the universe.

My wife yells,

"Steve, did you eat all the vegetable soup?" "Yes," I yell back.

The Dodgers won last night. Great game. Cathy, me
and the kids went, great night, but right now I'm a red
pepper ball, though I'm a little pissed off at my wife. She
used a tone with me when she asked if I ate the soup. The
soup was for someone else, I guess. How was I to know?
That tone, it bugs me. I am very sensitive to her tones.

My stomach tightens. I have to go to the bathroom and
for some reason, not having to do with anything, I realize
I am taken care of by more loving forces than I know. In
fact what I know is very little of any of it, but it's what I
have.

I smell parsley. My wife is cutting parsley. It smells green.

Give that to the blind man.

I'm not trying to say anything with any of these poems, which is itself something. I mean, it's a statement. Our kids don't want to eat anything so Cathy is making a fruit shake for them. That's something.

I don't have anything interesting to say. I'm feeling funny. Slightly malicious. Poetry is slightly malicious. It doesn't just like things the way they are, it has to go and draw attention to them.

Now my wife is making fun of our children and their never-satisfied whining.

She is feeling poetic too. Oh I love her more, now. Feel softness growing for her.

Good, I have been feeling distant recently. I try to get close and then she starts talking about God and chewing her food loudly and I have to leave the room.

I'd like to share God with her more, but it is so intense. She's having visions.

The wind comes through the window, rustles the papers on my desk. My wife is talking loud to me, from the kitchen, about her sisters and their Margaritas last night. I don't drink. I mean, if I do I'll destroy the whole thing, this life. The whole thing is far more complex and strange than I could have imagined. I mean love and wholeness. I mean when a guy really starts getting whole, good things start happening, I mean really good, peace and awareness things, aware that it's not all peaceful. No, the thing is here, right now, nothing is wrong. Okay, a little stress about the American Express bill. Gonna have to negotiate. But nothing wrong. Maybe it's just me. Maybe I'm lucky or it's cause I'm white and have a job, but everything is all right, even this funny feeling that I'm forgetting something, is all right.

I'm listening to the blender, looking at Proust—big books, those Proust books.

I get these big books just so I can stare at them and think about what they must be like to read and then I think of Jack Fris, my holy friend who reads all the big books, Infinite Jest, Mason & Dixon, Ulysses, and isn't full of shit or pretentious about any of it.

I'm sitting here without a metaphor in my pocket, without a pocket, in my gym shorts, which I slept in. It is 11:30 a.m. My daughter, Maya, calls me from the bathroom. Got to wipe her caca, no metaphors here. Though I have nothing against them, like chicken, just right now I'm not eating any and when I do only free range. I'm getting uptight eating habits. I haven't had a patty melt in a while. Only free range metaphors, metaphors grown the natural way, the way God intended, running around pecking at worms of life, hopping around the coop of my mind, running from the rooster, squawking when the dog comes near. Dog is God spelled backwards.

There is no way that this is a poem, but I'm calling it one anyway. I'm feeling malicious.

I'm cracking myself up here. Walt Whitman wrote his own reviews. Said some pretty great things about himself, in the third person. I'll try it. "He's a child of the western sun, a natural sun tan man. He's a Beatnik with new American shoes. I am American." America is pretty cool when you live in Echo Park in September, 2001.

Listen, what I wanted to say, what I thought I was going to say, is that the Dodgers won last night. That's it. Really. It's 11:37 a.m. The family went to the game. We watched the fireworks afterward, fan appreciation fireworks, but the Dodgers won. 3 to 2. Gagne got another save, #48. It was great watching him walk in from the bullpen. Everyone was screaming. I'm getting goofy teary-eyed thinking about it. He's a hero. And Dodger Stadium sits in the heart of the city. Chavez Ravine. I always try to picture what it looked like before, Chavez Ravine back in 1945, still and distant, remote and humble village of Mexican poverty. I always feel like I can see it, almost, not with eyes, but somewhere in my belly, I can see it with my guts and then I think of the school house buried under the pitcher's mound.

And I think, or thought, last night, with the sun going down, the sky dark mostly, with a burned orange lip above the horizon, fire season sunset, I thought, the Dodgers chose it right. I mean, they chose the heart of the city. It's all out there, spreading out beneath us, around us. And how sweet it would be if the city had un American secrets like Chavez Ravine still intact, by un-American, I mean not all together and profitable. And I think that the secrets I am speaking of really are inside us, always, never outside, never for long, or they are, but the point is, the secrets, the special moment of quiet light, when the world spreads out all around us and dinner, and telephones ringing and neighbors drunken singing, it's us, when Penelope asks all about the big yellow foul pole and the peanut guy calls her honey and the sun is gone, and the Chavez Ravine school yard bell rings with the Dodger's organ, when all that happens, it's us doing that. That's all I'm saying.

Lunch is ready.

SUNLIGHT PANTOUM

We are made of sunlight,
dangles of the forever glow.
We are illuminated bone,
love and wonder, outright and upset.

We are dangles of the forever glow.
We may not know that, but we are that.
We are love and wonder, outright and upset.
We are the yellingest bottles of bright rain.

We may not know that, but we are that.
Listen, the sun. It moves through us.
We are the yellingest bottles of bright rain.
We bear the proud electric, draw the rising day.

Listen, the sun. It moves through us.
We are its bright fingers, healing each other's storms.
We bear the proud electric. Draw the rising day.
Undo the hammer, the lying chains.

We are the sun's bright fingers, healing each other's storms.
Cure our broken water. Bring it to the day.
Undo the hammer, the lying chains.
Our breath is made of sun.

Cure our broken waters. Bring them to the day.
We hold the sunlight answer in this wound.
Our breath is made of sun. We are lit clay.
Shaped by the brightest hand.

We hold the sunlight answer in our wounds.
We are all the same light, the only one light,
shaped by the brightest hand.
We are all illuminated bone.

YOU CAN'T STOP IT, SO DON'T TRY—
PERSONAL POEM #9

It is a new year. 4:11 in the afternoon. This being
alive stuff is exhausting and I can't stop this poem from
going where it needs to go. I can't stop my heart beat, or
my breath, the water running through the pipes, the gas
in the wall, the birds flying, the toilets flushing, the music
coming out of Larry's window. I can't get Larry to work
on my car. He's been working on my car for one month. I
think he's pissed off at me.

What else can't I stop or start? Everything. Anything.
I can try and maybe I can stop my daughter from stapling
her finger, for now, but it's going to happen one day. I can't
stop my arm from twitching, my blood from sending little
boatloads of blood through my capillaries. I can't stop
my lungs from taking in air, using the oxygen, expelling
carbon dioxide. I can start the car, but really not even
that, it's not me. I'm just turning the key. That's all I can
do, turn the key.

This is freedom.

The truth is, we thought we were moving to the next
door neighbor's house and that she was selling it to us
for a good price, below the market. But her daughter and
son in law got involved and we are not going to buy it for
a good price. We are not going to buy it at all. They are

going to sell it for max value and start a bidding war and be part of the price gouge soul kill human lose real estate market. We can't afford this game. I am jealous. I am pissed.

Funny to think that I sat and stared at the over ripe bananas, thought about banana bread, thought about God and looked at her house and about this life being a house made of God and sat and listened and wrote a poem and thought that we could move into that house and then the old lady was gonna sell it to us, special gift from god and I thought that all life fit into the dream that I had of it. Ha ha. I can't buy the house next door. Can't scream and yell my way into the place. I tried.

"Ain't that a bitch." The seventies song is coming out of Larry's apartment. I think God is playing it for me. I'm pissed. God is a jerk. He's playing it because he's pissed off at me. I'm tired. I don't know why.

This is Freedom.

I sit around feeling what I'm feeling and I'm not doing anything about it, or trying not to, like burn the house down, shoot someone. My daughters are being brats to each other and I'm just watching the feelings and if they really get ugly I'll just feel it and stop them from getting really ugly, but I won't freak out. Let's see how long I can keep this up.

So we don't get the house. So things are changing. So who is next on the block? We just rent this place? So things change and who knows why? So hy do I write these things? So I can't make anything happen or not. So God doesn't sell houses. That's just what they are made of.

"Ain't that a bitch."

It's time to take Penelope to swimming lessons. I yell at her to put her suit on.

THE WEATHER IN MY MIND

The song says it's all in my head. I think about it.
The sidewalk's grey wet dewy concrete, the grass,
the roosters that call across the blue roofs of dawn,
even the clouds and cold air that scratches my nose as I sit here,
it's all in my mind, everything, starting
in the universal bean, the seed of factories and oceans.

Sitting here, looking at what's true, I'm scared of doing anything.
I'm not angry right now. It's nice.
Oh these mopey poems of love and tranquility, drunk on nothing,
everything, toasting the air with my bowl of soup,
my daughter, Maya, singing "I love weather and time,"
as she turns on the TV to see if it is going to rain.

THE POINT I AM TRYING TO MAKE

It is 12:10 p.m., Saturday, June 13th.

My daughters are yelling in the next room, playing a game called Shugi. Shugi is a dog. Maya is Shugi, Penelope is her master.

The sky is the color of yellow chalk, blue chalk like the chalk I used once to draw a bug on the sidewalk. Penelope and Maya were small.

It was a good bug. It rained the next day.

Chalky mud, the color of this 12:10 sky, was all that was left. I understood. It's difficult, but I understand, and it's still
    difficult.

I sold *The Book of Lies* to Brand Books. Aleister Crowley. When I was doing speed and watching pornography all night with my family asleep downstairs, I would read it, and understand it. Now, that I don't do speed or watch pornography while my family sleeps I can't tell you what the thing was about at all. It was all some kind of bullet in the head paradox, some kind of cryptic lost continent hangover.

Now I just think of the time. I mean, what time it is now.
    I feel time in my rib cage
talking to me like a bird looking for the land of velvet sunshine.

"It's almost the end of the world," says Maya, in the kitchen, talking to her mom.

"What do we do when it's the end of the world?" asks Cathy fixing the kids some frozen pizza for lunch. She is a good mom.

I hear Cathy and feel her lying next to me in bed. I think of sex, often.

I believe in the oblivion kiss.
I believe in execution by amnesia.
I look at photos Penelope whispering in her sister's ear.

Pictures of Maya with the beanie we bought from an Indian lady at the Zocalo in Mexico City back in 1996.

I think of Mexico City, blind man walking down ancient streets. Corona Beer neon Spectacular signs on the boulevard. Little birds pecking out pieces of blue paper that give you a fortune. A drunk guy selling a bag of Gillette razors, telling me his name is Michael Jackson. I want to go back to Mexico. Old guys pulled stuff on carts drawn by burros.

I remember Knott's Berry Farm Burro rides with my brother down around the Lagoon and grandma Duvall singing along to the songs playing at the Merry Go Round. Turkey in the straw. I was little like these kids of mine.

It is 1:50 p.m. Penelope calls her sister a big fat cheater. I look at the eye in tail of a peacock feather I have on my desk

and I think of heaven and think about my daughters
choosing to come down to us here.
The name calling is getting worse here.

    The sunlight is fragile and lovely.
I feel like an alien
because I'm so impressed.

    It is now 2:05, 2:06
and that is the point of this
after all. That is the whole point.
This is no lie.
This is the truth.

MEDITATIONS DURING THE NFC CHAMPIONSHIP

This is personal,
and easy.
The water is on, boiling, it's gonna start whistling.
When I'm at home, all I do is drink tea.
That's easy. Life is easy to look at. Moving around
That gets hard sometimes. We moved. My family.
We don't live in Echo Park anymore.
It's been a year and a bit. The NFC football
championship is on TV. The Marines are crying
at the National Anthem. Everyone is crying.
Saddam Hussein is crying, Osama Bin Laden,
crying. I am not crying.
I am looking at the green hills of El Sereno,
and the hazy San Gabriels behind them.
Moving is hard, was hard. Now I'm here.
That's easy. Our fence gets graffiti. The summer is hot here.
The ocean is far. I don't walk around the neighborhood,
too many ghetto dogs. I took the kids out for a walk once,
the dogs freaked us all out, little dogs running out of their yards,
big ones banging up against their fences, barking Gestapo
    shepherds,
loose ones, pit bull lost dog, sniffing shit,
but that's just dogs; the sky is good,
the hills, sweet, empty. I don't want to get too critical.
I want to keep up with my breathing. I mean stay right here.
Not get lost. This is our house, that's a cool thing.

You know, there's a bank involved.

The TV is off. My brother is in town, at a swimming meet,

He's a coach. Funny, he almost drowned at Gynx lake
when we were kids,

all I did was sit and watch. I thought he was funny, kidding around.

I was a kid myself, you know. I feel bad about it, so I remind myself

that I was just a kid. Still, I don't really get involved in
other people's

sufferings. Really, I just watch out for myself. I feel bad
about this, cause

I want everyone to be well, to do right, to not fuck with
me. Really, I do

get involved, now. If my brother was drowning now, I'd
get off my inner tube and swim to him. Still, when shit
goes wrong, my first reaction is to get mad

at whomever for having problems, for doing something wrong.

It's like when I was walking the kids through the
neighborhood and

all the dogs started freaking out and they started crying, I ended

up swatting Penelope in the butt, because she was scared
and freaking out.

You know, it was the Pull Yourself Together Goddammit
approach to well being.

But that was a year ago. I've looked into myself and seen the seed

of the unquiet. What is it? It is fear,

I fear my own lack of glue. Why? Why?

Cause without glue, I feel that I will die, be ripped apart

or fall apart, not live, not be full of sun, be hated,

fall to the bottom of hell shit pit of doom suck you lose your mind.

Yes, what a hell of moment that is. It comes,

brain injection of shit blood hate drip. How?
So fast, the freakout comes. Scream, cry, fear,
SHUT THE FUCK UP!! FUCK YOU, AAAAHH!!
What to do? Give up! Get in touch with your inner robot,
don't believe what your toxic blood stream brain telegraph
    is telling you.
Get into the sunlight inside your own box of human love.
Listen to the Beatles. Put the beach in your mind. See the Beatles
in other people.   See the sunlight that we all carry
like a bucket of glowing orange juice.
The glowing bucket of eternal vitamin C.
These things help. It is true.
But there are islands in me populated by Japanese soldiers
that don't know the war
is over. How do I get to them?
And when I get there then what?
I'm white, an American, the enemy.

It is one o'clock. I'm gonna check the score
of the game.

HEAVY THOUGHTS ON A HOT DAY

It's hot, thick hot heat, kind of frightening,
like it could make you into a marshmallow,
so I turn off the CD player
and turn on the fan.
Or do I turn off the computer.
That's what I am thinking about as I sit here.
I like to slouch when I type, spread out, toes way out.
Or sit over the typer, hunched over the thing,
or sit up straight, like I'm playing saxophone in a big band,
though I don't know how to play the horn,
this here set of lettered keys, that's my ax,
love me right now, feeling a little sun light in my natural belly.
I've got saxophone on the brain.
Listening to lots of Coltrane these last two days,
Parker right now.
I get up, look out the window; it is so hot, Lord, the heat
     wants to crush us all,
crush us, invaders, defilers, flowers, only the sand knows
     how to bathe in this heat,
be sand.

Penelope is sending me notes about how she misses her
old school, friends she's known since Pre School. She
signs her notes Mystery Girl. I write her back, tell her
yes, I know what you mean and yes, she is so full of love
and God, that she's gonna be so okay and do you wanna go

watch the sun go down. Maya is the mailman, which is the same thing, too. Be sand. Bathe in the heat. The heat of them. The horns. Let it all have you.

Spiritual Question: Since pain and pleasure are always part of the same coin, do I cease to attach to pleasure in order to get out of pain, or do I learn to see pain and pleasure as necessary aspects of the whole experience? I don't think I can love my daughters any less and feel the pleasure of this love any less, nor my wife, I can't love her any less. I didn't make this love up, it just is, it was given to me, it's a gift, so wadda I do?

Heavy thoughts on hot day.

The kid who lives next door, I looked at his comic book the other day. There was a young girl in a short skirt and the skirt is blowing up a little. It's horrible. Kids can't look at that. The thing is they can look at that cause they don't know what they are looking at. I mean, sure they do, but no they don't. I can't look at it cause I have problems. Or maybe he does know about this, sure he does, he just doesn't look like he does but he doesn't know what I know it means. He's little, eleven, and hasn't been ravaged by sexual addiction, face creased with lust and shame. That will come later. I mean, he hasn't had sex yet, he can't know what kind of sweet mind blown velvet house of galaxy lives beneath her skirt. No way, only old men like me know.

I have become much more open to my fucked-upness, recently. It has calmed me down. I'm not fighting. The heat is not just from the sun, you know. There are lots of suns, you know. Be sand.

EXCITEMENT AND CHINESE FOOD

I'm not excited right now.
I'm on my way to Chinese food with the family.
I've got a headache.

That's why Jack Kerouac
      Ted Berrigan
        and me all liked speed—
It makes you feel excited
about absolutely nothing or anything,
which is a great thing—it feels right,
symbolic, everything resonates, the metaphor
of life is clear. Metaphor for what?
The spiritual parable that is our very breath, man.
That's what.

But the speed eats your brain
and the happy excited symbolism
of amphetamine turns into
derelict psychosis as your body begins
to rot and the walls and their shadows say bad things
and everyone knows you're fucked
and they are saying so with every gesture they make.

Excitement, it's overrated
by the adolescent life judge
that lives in my mind.

He is an abused fellow, unable
to look at the more uncomfortable
things in life.

I am at Chinese food, Phoenix Inn,
me and the family, doing well,
dealing with hunger discomfort,
the upset from me messing up our new cement steps.
I stepped on the edge, it was wet, it crumbled,
so I suck.

Penelope watches me close,
waiting to see if I will freak.
I acknowledge this in her, in me.
I think it will help the process.
It helps break up the block of ice
that is unspoken discomfort.

Now my cements steps are more like me.

The food is arriving. Pea leaves in garlic, rice.
Joe, the waiter, loves my daughter Maya
and her egg drop soup.

Penelope asks me if I want rice.
I'm writing this whole time.
Family in the corner, loud, talking Chinese.

"What do homeless people do when they die?" Penelope
    asks. Deep girl.

So excitement,
what about it?

I'm hungry.
I'm gonna eat now.
That's what.

CITY DAWN SONNET

We wake up in this city, the sun opening
doors and engines, drawing us into the noise
of freeways, growing out of the sky. We dream
broken. We move through the day looking for grace,
for gold, for soldiers, for a purse of solid reason.
We aren't smart. We live in boxes of fear,
pasting the walls with pictures of where we pretend
we are, would like to be. We are our walls, scars
of golden rifle pipelines under the sea. Chained
to the absence of the things we desire.
Looking for our light in the lamps of lost trains.
The freeways fill up, widen, the machines require it,
demands our hands be held to our failures.
Somehow the sun seems to have seen it all before.

THE STEAM ROLLER

I am alive,
and alive is about
taking turns.
It was my turn to be 18,
and 20, and 27, now 39.
The thing is, I thought
I was driving, I was
driving the world.
I thought the whole world was at
my bowling alley birthday party,
It didn't matter what was
true and real.
Now, now
the steam roller called reality
is on me, paving streets that
I never heard of.

THE ASSHOLE POEM

It's July 31st,
It's after 11 p.m., just.
I'm in Berkeley, California, slightly
obsessed with Ted Berrigan. His
wife, the only female poet I am
enthusiastic about. That's bad,
I know. I know. I should be
enthusiastic about Louise Gluck,
Adrienne Rich, but Alice Notely
moves me. She's secret.

We are about honesty, here, filling the page with finger
    print words.

In the car, right now, I was brilliant, words and lines like
    meditations, presence,
vision, hanging from my eyes and the bodies and the lights
    and the shadows
of Shattuck Avenue. Now, I can't remember a thing.

What I want to say, honestly, with poetry, vision,
    inspiration and art
sputtering all around me like sand crabs digging holes in
    the newly gone tide,
is that I am an asshole and I am sorry for snapping at my
    wife today in San Francisco on the J train.

I had a good day today with the family in San Francisco,
saw the Chagall retrospective, and saw a show, a
    retrospective of a man named
Phillip Guston. A discovery for me, like discovering
    sunlight. Chagall was cool,
lovely, Chagall, of course, but Guston was there. I mean
    the man was
present in his work. I mean his spirit, his ghost was there,
    angel of paint brush vapor,
essence of rust, nails, cigar smoke crucifixion halo. What
    mossy headdress did
yon apparition wear? He was there directing us all to the
    pain and moment in each canvas.
Chagall, I think, has returned to life as a cat, or a verse of poetry,
but Guston was there weeping on the floor, joy tears, blood water.
I was breathing out poems when I walked through his canvases.

Okay, need a new word for spirit, one not bleached by the new age.
One that speaks of the invisible present/presence of holy
    anger and love
bodies, breaking open the fruit within, personal trees
    between us all.
What is that?

The point is the day was good but
I was just an asshole, for about 3 minutes, a minute, 90
    seconds, and that
really fucks with the other 1437.

I'm not trying to be funny here. I'm just trying to get up
     front about everything.
I told my wife she was retarded.
She looked retarded on the F train carrying
the kids' bottles of Gatorade in her purse. We all got on the
     crowded F in San Francisco.
The driver saying kindly the kids are only thirty-five cents
     and me not having
thirty-five cents, just dollars. Cathy, do you have thirty-five
     cents?
She digs through her purse.
It was so sad watching her dig through her purse. What is
     it about her purse?
Her and her purse? Why is it so sad, her digging through
     her purse? I was whacked out on Ghiradelli's chocolate
     sundae and she was the universe searching for itself
     inside
a dark and Q-tip market receipt filled purse in San
     Francisco.
The noise, the people, no seats, Maya sitting on the floor,
tired legs, defenseless tourists in The City,
and she, so humble and earnest, looking for thirty-five
     cents. And me waiting with
all this sadness. Sorrow is always the body beneath angers
     horrible face. Why so sad? Why angry at sadness?
 She found it, but I was already heartbroken. I couldn't just
     fall apart there. No, so
I got mean and said bitterly, with poison, trying to mask
     the heartbreak
of her pureness, or the world's silliness, the cruelty of

thirty-five cents, a great day with
the family, really, no shit, no irony, a great day, but it's cruel
   just the same,
because they end, like everything, and you want to pound
   the floor, stay, no stay, and I looked at the Gatorades
   sticking out of her purse, ridiculous and awkward
   paraphernalia of motherhood, children's drinks bought
   because the kids cry and whine and it's not the worst
   thing they could want but of course they only drink a
   mouthful and then you are carrying them in your purse
   or jacket pocket, a smart-
looking bag meant for discreet items, keys, a compact, a
   hidden mess perhaps,
but not the tops of Gatorade bottles, Lemon Lime and
   Fruit Punch flavor,
no that is too naked, too on the run. I can't live like that.
   Not with eternity
coming down all around us, the German tourists and the
   train man watching,
down here at Fisherman's Wharf.

I'm tired. Tired of myself. Tired of my attempts to make
   art out of neurosis, rage, addiction, disease.
But my throat is twinkling, little men inside of me are
   laughing. I am funny to them. Who are they? I think
   they are responsible. And I am sorry for saying "You
   really look retarded. Here, let me take those and put
   them in my bag." (I hide them in my newly purchased
   City Lights 50th anniversary book bag, which marks
   me as a different kind of tourist).

My wife looks at me. She wants to cry. She is vulnerable.
She is as open hearted as the sky. She wants to kill me,
too, of course. Like life. Love is so thin and fragile, like
breath and just as enduring. She just stands there and
says nothing. Looks at me. "What? It's true. Let me
take those, they look retarded."

Someone on the trolley stinks of alcohol. The driver, I
think. His copy of the New Testament propped up in
the window. His kindness, frantic, pleading. "Please,
please, step up the stairs. We can count the money on
the trolley."

JACK IN THE BOX CHILD, MIDNIGHT, 1985

I am the walleyed child
with the swollen ear,
staring at your face
as if it were a starry sky and I a young Joshua Tree
tangling arms into you.
I smell your cold
planets lurking in the trunk.
I know their longing for narcotic ticker tape flora.
I can't help you.
I don't have the key
to your seed, anywhere.
I have scoured the walls of your hatred.
The Towering Inferno still burns for all of us.
I was there on the movie theatre floor with you
and your forgotten brother.
Giant Robot died. The only machine who cared.
Poison was the answer
the dog man gave me.
My mother was a coat of blown leaves left on a car lot fence.
My father was a burning tire, rolled down the alley into traffic.
I am the tyrant philosopher of your
errored liberation.
I don't have any reasons,
I just stare at you
like a broken egg.
I know you

understand all of this.
You made me
in a half milk carton
put in Ms. Thoman's second grade window sill.
You watched me grow and stop like a comma
hanging in the air—aluminum fish. Broken Astronaut visions.
I don't know why you never talked to me.
I waited there for years. Both hands flying after you,
pointing to the sun, but you insisted on other things.
Do you even remember that?
Probably not.

PISSED OFF AT NOTHING

I am watching the kids tonight, while Cathy is at her third eye session with Gautama, the therapist. Right now, I am tired and getting over being pissed off at nothing, which is how I spend most of my day, but an hour ago I took out the garbage and felt heaven in the rainy fog and dark sky, Standard Time, dark by six, a kind darkness, Echo Park street lights, orange dots, Larry's TV on next door, flickering blue window. Dark dirt lot. I can see him walking around in his apartment. The kind and gentle alcoholic closet case mechanic, at least that is what I see

Right now, it is 7:38, November 8th; time is a habit. The World Series is long over. The Angels have finally won. The pretty poverty of Echo Park is expensive. But things are not what I am amazed by. I am amazed by the breath within the things, amazed by the sounds we make and then cry over. What are these sounds, words, words, fart, nothing. What are we really crying over? What is really going on? It is the breath in things. That's what's going on.

I am getting freaky here. I feel good. I feel my arms, my fingers. My heart smiles when I stop and feel my arm and fingers and neck. It really does. I will just follow the smile.

The night right now, is so full of me. It knows me.

Why do I say this? It feels like that. The night knows me, everything knows me, me and everything, we are tight, we know each other, we are the same. You, you out there, you are made for me, whoever you are, how does it feel? And you there in the night, cause when you read this it will be night, I am made of you, sleeper, brother, sun breather.

Heaven is out of control.

It is swimming in my green carpet and my black shoes.

Act Natural, it warns me.

I go turn the stove on, another cup of tea. Chamomile this time.

I wonder what time Cathy will come home.

We cry cause it all hurts.

PISSED OFF AT NOTHING, AGAIN

I'm upset. I don't feel good. Not my favorite time to write.

I'm tired of feeling bad, of not feeling good.

Things on my mind: UCLA plays SC in football at noon. I have to work on a paper. There are too many kids at my school who are spiritually damaged ball-headed punks. I think I'm an asshole. My wife is psychic and I'm not. I came home the other day and she was sharing her psychic spiritual experience with a brother-in-law and I feel like an asshole, hairy ape. I'm jealous. I feel left out. It's embarrassing. Jack Kerouac gives me permission to be embarrassing in a piece of literature, but in life, who gives me permission for that.

Spiritual for me is just being able to breathe and not fucking freak out.

I want to be enlightened. I want to know something that will make me know that I'm not worse or better than anyone. What is that? When I did speed I felt that way, for a day, the rest of the time, just lost and poisoned. Actually, I felt better than everyone. Actually, I still think I am better than everyone. No chance for peace.

Shit, there's this sad flower opening up in my chest. It just keeps getting bigger and bigger.

I want to say something good. I want it all to be good. Work the program. Pray. Open up, breathe, let go. True. True. I'm safe here. That's all I want: eternal safety. But time is ripping me to shreds as I sit here. 10:52 and fiftyseven seconds, 10:53. There I go.

Brahmachary, Brahmachary—this word keeps ringing in my head. I read it in Seymour, An Introduction. What does that mean? I'll look it up in Eastern Philosophy for Beginners.

I want what everyone else has. I don't want what I have, because I already have it. Who needs that?

I'm folded. I'm sparrow. I'm bones. I'm bottoming out on my own bullshit.

Thanksgiving is next weekend. I am hopeful. I hate hope.

It means that I'm not here. God, it's all over. I can't run from any of me anymore.

Thanks. Thanks. Eventually, I'll be gone and I'll learn something. Something will be learned.

SUCKS

Beginnings suck.
Waking up sucks.
Being finite creatures with infinite hungers sucks.
Not really being an infinite creature but thinking you are sucks.
Being starlight lovely in a rat turd world sucks.
Being full of shit sucks.
Hatred sucks.
cause it's always there.
Happiness sucks
cause it ends.
Ends suck.
Sorrow sucks.
Poetry sucks.
Wanting to be famous sucks.
Wanting to be a famous poet sucks.
Bitterness sucks.
Money sucks.
Money sucks cause there is never enough.
Never enough sucks.
All human needs controlled by capitalist greed sucks.
Change sucks.
Intelligence sucks.
Famous writers suck.
Echo Park sucks.
Duck shit sucks.
Water sucks.

White people suck.
Black people suck.
Mexican people suck.
America sucks.
Hurricanes suck.
Racism sucks.
America's racist power structure sucks.
Benefiting from the racist power structure sucks.
Not benefiting from the racist power structure sucks.
Living in an Emperialist world fucking nation corporation sucks.
Not living in one sucks.
Shopping at Costco sucks.
Feeling good about shopping at Costco and being
    surrounded by so much product and having that make
    you feel good, safe, secure—that sucks.
Dead bodies suck.
Rape sucks.
Murder sucks.
Birth sucks.
Sunday sucks.
Chinese food sucks.
Piss smell sucks.
Hip hop sucks.
Ranchero music sucks.
Rock 'n Roll sucks.
The Beatles suck.
Run DMC sucks and have sucked.
The Sex Pistols sucks.
The Germs sucks.
The Beat Generation sucks

Allen Ginsberg sucks.

Marriage sucks.

Children suck—they suck the life right out of you.

Loving your kids so much you want to kill yourself
because they keep changing and growing and time
never stops—that sucks.

Sitting there looking at them, thinking what happened,
where did it all go, the time, the years, where was I,
sucks.

Wondering if you did a good job, or a good enough job, sucks.

Thinking that you wasted a lot of time trying to write
world famous poems sucks.

Parents suck—alcoholic, super depressed, and broken
furniture raging maniacs in their

underwear when you come home from the movies—
parents completely suck

Constantly writing about them, trying to skewer them in
ranting verse, sucks.

Trying to vomit out the bullshit beliefs they fed me sucks.

Trying to learn how to love and trust people sucks.

Love and trust suck.

No, love and no trust suck, and suck hard with teeth.

Sex sucks.

No sex sucks more.

Masturbating sucks.

Masturbating and getting toxic porno imagery stuck in
mind and sore penis the day after great celestial sex
with soul mate sucks.

Masturbating thinking that no sex with soul mate will
happen in near future only to find out that soul mate is

indeed feeling very sexy sucks.

Soul mate not thinking you are soul mates after all sucks.

School teachers suck.

School sucks—mediocrity factory, originality stared at as if a fish flopping around on a pier, boxed minds, waste of money, kids eating shit for lunch and throwing it at weird kid.

PE sucks.

Asshole 12-year-olds making fun of the hair that grows in the teacher's nose suck.

Students' kids calling you, the teacher, "fag" sucks, especially if you're an adult male who is insecure about being humiliated by future Gestapo Jail Guards or inmates.

Insecurity sucks.

Humiliation sucks.

Torture sucks.

Jail sucks.

Guards suck.

Freedom sucks.

You suck.

I suck.

We suck.

They suck.

All pronouns suck.

Your momma sucks.

Your daddy sucks.

Wednesday sucks.

Jesus sucks.

Jehova sucks.

Church sucks, totally and completely—fascist God, idiots
    talking about eternity as if it wasn't eternal, learning
    more about truth and god watching pornography and
    developing a sexual addiction and a coke problem.
    That sucks.
Sexual addiction sucks.
Drug addiction sucks.
Recovery from sex and drug addictions suck, but it's better
    than being fucked up on porno and crystal.
Masturbating till you bleed sucks.
Heroin sucks.
Amphetamine sucks.
Rent sucks.
Ownership of property sucks.
Real estate agents suck.
Gangsters suck.
Gangster real estate agents suck.
Planet earth sucks.
The sun sucks.
Duhomie West Africa sucks.
Nazis suck.
Israel sucks.
Loneliness sucks.
No one home sucks.
Porno sucks; we've already talked about that. That sucks.
Only fucking when your wife wants to sucks.
Fucking when she doesn't want to sucks more.
Emotionally empty and resentful fucking sucks.
Repetition sucks.
Editing sucks.

Saying this sucks sucks.
Giving a shit sucks.
The psychic wound sucks.
The Astral wound sucks.
Past life wounds suck.
Past life sucks.
This life sucks.
Your kids telling you to "shut up" sucks.
Telling your mom to fuck off sucks.
Opening up to cosmic and pure and inescapable sorrow sucks.
Suicide sucks.
Buddha sucks.
Suffering sucks.
The Eight Fold Path sucks.
Tatoos suck.
Regret sucks.
Tattoos of regret suck.
Soul mates suck.
Soul mates that leave suck.
Fucking around on your soul mate sucks
Knowing someone who is fucking around on their soul
    mates sucks.
I haven't done it; that sucks.
Thinking I should do it, even for a second, sucks—sucks bad
Should sucks.
Should not sucks.
Driving sucks.
Freeways suck.
Asphalt covering the planet and all living things sucks.
White man kicking nature's ass sucks.

Kicking ass sucks.

Nature sucks.

Nature kicking man's ass sucks.

Having high blood pressure sucks.

Having to take care of yourself sucks.

Having a heart attack sucks.

Exercise sucks.

Walking sucks.

Society stuck on destruction of the very things that feed it sucks.

Capitalism sucks.

Communism? We will never know.

Fanatics suck.

Hedonism sucks.

Puritanism sucks.

Hipsters at the Brite-Spot suck.

Hipsters taking over a neighborhood you once felt pure and home and real estate agents gouging and gouging and driving the home prices so high into insane greed buggered asshole range sucks.

Believing that hipsters actually raised the property value sucks.

Art as a force of gentrification sucks.

Racism disguised as Neighborhood Improvement sucks.

Echo Park Historical Society sucks.

Families living for generations in a neighborhood and then being displaced by greedy personal trainers and costume designers who are most likely going to leave the house in less than five years sucks.

Rich people taking over the park with their fucking fancy dogs suck.

Stepping in their dog shit sucks.

Yelling at them sucks.

Having some psycho yell back at you and threaten to kick
  your ass in front of your family sucks.

Never getting over having to move from a place you loved sucks.

Not really wanting to live there anymore sucks.

Not admitting you're happier where you are now than
  you've ever been sucks.

Avant garde jazz sucks.

Accomplishment sucks

Being an artist sucks .

Discipline sucks.

"It sounds good, but how does it work on paper?" sucks

"Get up and go" "Go get 'em" "Carpe Diem" suck.

Wet-noodle-thinly masked depression sucks.

"Fuck the world" sucks.

Success sucks.

Successful friends suck even more.

Free loader friends suck.

Being a slob sucks.

Realizing you're a slob sucks.

Realizing that you're not so fun to be with sucks.

Marijuana sucks, sucks ass, stupidest drug on the planet.

Beer sucks. It's good, but it sucks.

Crystal meth sucks, oh so bad.

Lying to yourself about it sucking, that sucks oh so worse.

Losing your teeth sucks.

Poverty sucks.

Poor people suck.

Hunger sucks.

Ronald Reagan sucks.

George Bush sucks.
John Kerry sucks.
Bill Clinton sucks and gets sucked and that's why W is President!
Illusive truth sucks.
The answer in a grain of sand sucks.
People who say they possess it suck.
Parents suck, again.
Compromise sucks.
Being a dickhead sucks.
Nice asses suck.
Great tits suck.
Big dicks suck.
Cute guys suck.
Gay men suck.
Straight people suck.
Lesbians suck.
Bravery sucks.
Being a pussy sucks.
Having so much money you can buy whatever you want
    sounds cool but it sucks.
Just barely having enough money to make ends meet sucks.
Just barely not having enough sucks, sucks bad.
Nirvana sucks.
Old ladies suck.
38-year-old poet teacher beatnik bitter asses suck.
Skinny hippy jesus dudes and the hot chicks who dig them suck.
Armenian goomba dudes with lighters snapping so cool,
    they suck.
Suck sucks.
Having a big ego sucks.

Having any kind of ego sucks.
Having to lose your ego to be happy sucks, but that's the
    way it is.
Being cool sucks.
Being really mad sucks.
Rage sucks.
Peace sounds cool, but it probably sucks too, how would I know.
Green trees and blue skies suck.
Houses you can't afford suck.
Afford sucks.
"Face it" sucks.
AIDS and dead friends suck.
Guns suck.
Golf sucks.
This could go on forever sucks.
It won't.
That sucks, too.

EL SERENO POEM

The night unfolds itself outside.
I'm inside. I can't see it, but I know it's out there,
through the window. Night, I am up late again, 2 a.m.
Doing work, grading papers, Thanksgiving weekend,
The end of a year is near. The fall brings colder winds,
lifting pieces of roof off the houses around town. That is symbolic.
I want to be a good person. I want to bring the light.
Hey, night, can I carry the light?
Night, you don't answer. It's okay. It's late. You
got other things on your mind, I know, it's like when my
kids ask me things and I'm deep into something else,
thinking about other things. I know.

It's quiet here,
listening to the specials. A message to you, Rudi.
A car just drove down the alley. El Sereno.
Leonard Cohen, singing about God.
My head is about to fall off, I am so tired.
I just had to write something to the night.
Hallelujah Night.

Oh, I need to be the adult around here. I can't be getting pissed
when my kid talks to me like I'm a retard. Hard. Very hard.

I want it all to work out. I want it all to be all right.
The world is not far away, My life is not a dream.

It is a thing, a deed. Right here. Life. I have to be real.
It is hard for me to be real.
How'd it happen? It just happened.
I asked for some things, from my soul guts.
Got them, said yes a few times and here I am.
In love, don't get me wrong.
I don't want my kids to read this and think it ain't good,
    that I didn't love them
or something like that, it's just that this is different.
The magic water, the dark bottle of stars that I
held inside me, that I drank from, that I followed
like it was a harpsichord being played on
a street with naked promises that only I could hear,
it seemed so beautiful, like it had all the truth, all the
    broken truth,
that I would ever need, and
I don't know what happened to it. I thought it was real.
I got scared I would die without God near
And really I guess this was the promise.
The truth is, I am happy with my belly digesting tuna fish,
Listening to the Carter family now, I Never Will Marry.
I'm not trying to be funny, just personal. The magic
bottle of water, the golden hound of purity.
I have never owned a dog,
but I love this one that is near me now.

Hey, Night, Hallelujah, pictures of my girls are all over my walls.
Halloween 2003, a witch and a fairy.
Oh we work ourselves into each other's lives so deeply.
I mean, I look at them and love them so much. It tears a

whole the size of you, night,
Right into my gut, soul. I thank you for that.
This is the bottle of stars, box of suns.

It all becomes so clear when you listen to the right song
over and over again.
I am being devoured.
I have never been happier in my whole life.

I HAVE BEEN ALIVE SO MANY TIMES

I have been alive so many times.

It is a great sorrow to be alive,
it is a great sorrow that opens us to God and truth,
which is the same thing,
and which is not sad? I don't know.
You'd think I'd know the way I carry on,
but I don't.

Why are we alive, after all? What is the point of this thing?
Why do I get so angry?
Why am I so hurt?
Will my daughters be okay?
Why does she cry in the night? Last night?
Is it my fault?
Why are my parents so sad and messed up?
What is the meaning of parents? Why do we have them?
Why do we need to deal with them? Is it all their fault?
I think so.
I am a parent.

Why are we living in this house?
Why this neighborhood?
We looked at so many houses over time,
over the years and we ended up here.
It was one of the better houses.

Why do I think about all the places we could have lived?
Why do I think that I fucked up, thinking about all the
   places we could have lived?
Why am I not famous? Why am I not great?
Why haven't I published another book after The Bus?
Why am I writing Johnny Future?
Why am I a beatnik? I was born in '67, should be punk
   rock, but liked disco
and popularity as a young person.
Why do I like punk rock now, a little, now that it is safely
   twenty years gone?
Why do I regret? Do I get something out of it?
I am happy with my wife. I mean, I don't think that there
   was another, better that I should have had.
I am in love with my children. Why do I yell at Penelope?
   She is so beautiful, such a spirit.

Penelope, you are such a spirit, so full of life and great
   things. You are love, made out of it purely and purely.

Why am I here, writing these things?
Why do I want to be a writer?
Why don't I think I am a writer?
What is a writer? Someone else, not me.
Someone successful, listened to, respected,
not me.
Why the feel sorrow for myself trip.
Why the dis-ease, the disease, why the
drugs and alcohol, why the sex obsessions,
why the pain that goes with them,

111

why not peace? Why not okay, why not
be like the sky, open and everywhere?
Why not the tree? Okay, I say okay to this.

How to be like the sky? The tree?
I am like the car, in need of repair,
needing to be filled with fuel every week or three days,
depending on how many trips across town I have taken.

Why am I better feeling (and looking, says wife)
at the beach?
How come I am poor and cannot live anywhere near the beach?
Why does the world hate poor people so much as to leave them
dying in desert looking for work borders to nowhere?

Why does my heart feel so sad, so bad, and why do I like it?

Allen Ginsberg, you are with me here, in the sunroom, my
    daughter in the shower,
my wife on the couch, the sun coming, chanting, heat, heat
    and more heat.
It is the end of August, good-looking people are ruining
    the world
and I want to be good-looking.

Why are all the secret stashes of humanity being sold for
    such high prices?
Why doesn't the TV ever go off?

What is on the TV now, a drama, someone dying?

Why do we die? Whose idea was that?
Are we supposed to get something right while we are here?
Is there a point to it? The poison hurts. I don't get
    anything out of it.
Will my bones be treated nicely?
Will my ashes find their way into the wild flowers? (My
    wife's idea, from a plane. I like it. Remember this.)

Why words on paper, why read Shakespeare, why care
    about immortality?
Art is immortality; why art? Why make?
The earth is doomed, we are just moss on a rock, a planet,
sending love to detention because it is out of uniform,
you know what I mean? Love is in detention.
Love should not be in detention.
Why is it in detention?
Who cares how the poem is shaped?
The red giant will swallow us whole, time will
melt our complexities—city water way magazine TVs on
    all night, (I have said it all before) all our detention
    rooms, all our rules, all our ins and outs,
melted by time around the sun…then what? Yes, then what?
Back to pure spirit clothes, gone looking for another body
    to learn in?
Bodies are hard to come by.

They feel good. They are feeling machines.
A question is a feeling? Yes, but that's not it.
Red and green bottles in the window.
Things. We need them. We are them.

Yes, but not really, not truly, not yessly true;
colors, we have them, love them, but not
really, the whole body is a question,
filled with questions, and one piece of knowing.

I have no arms, silly, of course I do, I can't park special.
It is hot. My kids are yelling, humanity
sparking in the sunlight, as me, dad lump,
bangs around the keyboard.

Thinking, looking around for the next word.
Back to the beginning, let the process show,
the wheels, the gears, the mind inside the wave,
why do I think this is a poem?
Why do I think anyone wants to hear what I have to say?
I don't have anything to say?
Just lots of questions?
And none of them for sale?
Are any of them for sale?
I'd like to sell something.
Here, take this, you the imagined reader,
the one who sees, the witness, god, the truth,
you always riding along, watching, in my own eyes,
a piece of heaven, why isn't it all heaven?
Why do we do this?
There is another way.
Who wants it? Do you?
Does anyone know how to get out of here?
Jim Morrison? Darby Crash,
he named himself. I didn't name myself.

Time named me, in the hands and minds of parents.
It is their fault, or they passed it on to me, now the fault
is all my own. I just want to let off a couple of
fireworks of mind while in this river, stream, floating to
    the ocean,
just the kind that flower, then stink, and spiral smoke
into the night, and you feel like that.

Will I like this tomorrow?
Will I even be here tomorrow?
I think I will, though I am insured.
That seems impossible. How can I not be here?
I have always been here. I will always be here.
How can I not be here? I made this place. My mind is all
    over it.
Sex keeps us here, keeps me here.
I am gonna want it today. Wanting is the beginning of
    form, bodies.

I think here is bigger than I think.

It doesn't matter if you don't believe me.
It doesn't matter if I don't know what I am talking about.
This is all true and international.

The cat stink rises from the pavement in the heat,
invisible, now gone.

That should be the end. That should end this thing.
You have somewhere else to go. You need to eat lunch,
or maybe go to sleep.
I rub my eye, scratch my whisker jaw. My hair is slightly greasy,
my back is sweaty. It is 11:16am here, August, hot.
The U.S. Open starts on Monday.
I want to end with something about my life, all of my lives,
the idea I started with.
I want some closure here, to reassure you and me both,
that I know what I am doing, but more than that to
reassure us that there is a form to this whole thing
that we understand, to some degree, and that, well,
to believe that there is closure, that things make
some kind of sense,
it's scary without that,
you know.

FORGOTTEN

All will be forgotten.
All this effort and bluster and try and do and be,
all this was and worry and wonder,
all this dust and tremble, all this must and will,
all the want and hurry, all this listing, still,
the list calms me in the face of forgetting.
The sound of my voice touches the essence now.
The word is so fragile, the symbol of the beginning,
God's big speaking, only God is remembered,
but then when this dust goes, he will be forgotten
and emptiness will hold it all, emptiness.
Oh flesh and sorrow at the end,
it is what you were made for.
You can't help it. You can't want it,
but you can't help it.

ODE TO ZERO

Oh, you who mean nothing,
eternal and hollow,
taking up space like breath,
or like time, moving things
over, from place to place.
You, marking each passage
of the cycle. You are
home-base, the egg,
the circle, the whole,
the hole, where all begins
again and again,
futilities' donut,
Hopes' smile.

We can never move
beyond nothing; all
roads lead to another
zero.
Oh, zero,
you are not one,
yet you are inside of one
and two, infinities
empty mirror.
Truly you are God's big eye.
You will never satisfy
my need to know how much you are,

but you cannot disappoint
because you promise
nothing,
and you are
nothing,
no and on.
In a million there are six of you,
holding the one way up into the sun.
You hold everything up.
But when I hold you, it's just air, my hand.
Are you holding me up?
How many of you are there
inside of me?

Zero, from which all comes
to which all goes
behind everything,
Ultimate and primary,
Silent, final, grave and womb,
You are kind,
Remembering nothing,
embracing everything.
We are more
like you than any other number,
hollow, holding up God knows what,
spitting out sums of love.

Zero, you are
the only number
that rolls.

MY FATHER DIED, OCTOBER 10TH, 2008

Dad, you have left your body.

I miss you. Yes. I do.
But then again, I have missed you for quite some time.
You have been gone for years, and the years that you were here,
well, they weren't always great.

I should only say lovely things. I should only speak of your
    greatness;
and to be sure, you were great. You were the oak tree, the
    ocean. You were a big man.
You were the fucking sun. And now you are dead. Now
    you are dead.
The sun is dead, the ocean, the big tree. Dead.
We all die, man. That is all there is to it.
We all die, man.
I am too tired for art. All I can do is write the shit.

I love you. I love you. But what does that mean?
Really, I love you. I love you. I love you.
But what does that mean?

Within your absence, a slow roar grows
like a train coming from out of the night
to be no more.

It is three days since you died.
Jerry said they went to the next room
and you just didn't wake up when they
came back. What did you know, old man. What did you know?
So tired, so tired, like bones carrying all of the ocean,
so much in the water that you just couldn't see
any more land?   What was it like, man?
What was it like? Oh, man, father, your body
had plans for you that you did not, that none of us do.
What final dream hands came to you,
hands made real.

Ha, feel that, feel that, all of us.

They go. They go. The ones you never thought
would go. They go.

I never thought you'd go.
I never thought you'd go.
What bullshit. I knew you were going.
But I never thought you would.

I tried to imagine it about a thousand times.
I knew you were dying years ago.
It was obvious. How could anyone think
otherwise? The only reason you lived was because
my mom wanted you to live. She wanted you
to live more than you did.
I knew you were dying.
We all did.

When you slid down the stairs, I thought
that was it. I cried. Read poetry to you.
You didn't die. I felt gypped.

Now, you did it. Now you went
and
and
and
it's not what I thought cause
death is not a thought.
What is it? Say it, Mr. Poet.
It is not a thought.
It is a body without the time
to be a body anymore.
It's the last page, gone.
Vagabond Soul.
Hummingbird Beloved.
King of the Cannery.
A Love Supreme.
Black Spring.

Everyone is dead.
Paul Newman.
Kurt Vonnegut.
Great people.
The guy who invented something great, I can't remember what.
he died.
A colleague from work's father, too, last week.
Open the paper. In the back of the California Section.
Right before the weather.

It's what we do.
It's what I am doing.
Body, body, body.
Body, body, body.
Body, body, body.
You are so funny.
I paint you with tattoos and I want a nice stomach.
But you are gonna kill me.
You are gonna fucking kill me.
Why? What have any of us ever done to you?
Besides not listen?

You see, Dad, father, Ralph Marvin,
This isn't about you.
It's about all of this.
You made us hamburgers that one time. Thank you.
I met you for dinner at the Old World Coffee Shop,
Santa Monica and 4th street, 1985. I was seventeen. That
    was so great.
Eating with you, meeting you, I don't remember the
circumstances. Why was I the only one there?
We talked about stuff. I felt old, grown up.
There were lots of shitty things, too.
But, that was your problem. You were a beautiful man.
I played your Thelonious Monk record, the one with
    "Abide With Me"
as the first track. You loved that cut. The sweet horns in harmony.
I listened to it yesterday. Abide With Me
Abide With Me. Is that what you are doing?

I keep getting this funny feeling of freedom,
like I am free from your bullshit.
Like you can't hurt me anymore.
That's funny. You were so out of it for so long,
but I still felt like I was supposed to do something and
you were always judging or something.

This last summer, you were so weak. I really felt you near
    the end.
But you were so kind, so aware, alive, your spirit so
    present and warm.
Even without words or much movement, it was present.
It's funny, we don't really communicate with words or movement.

I'm sorry you died. Not really, but it's the closest thing to
    what I want to say.

Body of Father, you are no more.
Eyes open, last words to me,
"Oh, okay."
I said " I'm going back to L.A. I'll see you this weekend."
And you said "Oh, okay."
I knew I was lying. I had to say something.
You were a man, a child, asleep, waking from dreams
    where you had to put things away but no time.
I swear, I thought you had passed a few times while I was
with you. Mouth open, head down, not moving. I had to
    look close to see
if you were still breathing. But then I left, and five days later,
you were gone. God bless you. I will freak out, I think,

when I see you,
dead body full of chemicals in the box of oak.
You oak tree of my life. I said that before, I know.
I mean it. You were a big tree in my life. Something to climb
and live under and look up to and just think of as life,
the undeadest thing that could ever be, freaking out.
You—wild man, gargantua of life, not death, you were the
    Life Man,
The Penis, which I think you had a big one. The Male
    Prinicipal. Rage Man.

Grandma came to Jerry in his mind, he heard her say,
"Marvy, come home."
The last thing I said to you
"I'm going back to L.A., Dad. I'll come back this weekend."
I knew that wasn't gonna happen.
I could have said something deep.
But what?

I want to watch TV.
I want to sleep.
I don't want to think about any of this.
Oh, but it wants to think about me.

I always say we live forever,
and we do, but the body—it's gone.
The finality, the lastness, that's
the hard part. Harder than the sickness.
The sickness is no good, it has to end, but
the end—it just doesn't forgive at all.

Shit, we hear about it.
We say I'm sorry for your loss,
but what are we really saying,
and what the fuck are we pretending?
That this stuff only happens to other people,
those less fortunate? Like we live in a good neighborhood
where people don't get sick and all those poor suckers—
I feel bad for them and their dying. Too bad they do that.
Poor assholes.

I'm sorry that you had to deal with the fact that is this life.
I'm sorry that you had to face the truth and had to stop
the fantasy illusion dream trip of invention and commerce. We
die, man. We die.

Dad, again you are my teacher, primary, primal, always
you, chosen by the cosmos to show me
the way into, through and now out
of this life.

REST STOP SONNET

I pull in, it's the middle of the night,
my family's sleeping in the car. I go
to pee and wash my face. There is a lantern
burning in one of the RVs parked
for the night. I look at it and ask, "Why
is there a lantern burning in an RV?
Those things have lights?" and I nod to myself,
the cars, the planted trees. Something's up
in there. There is something happening
between two people, or maybe one. Something
not for everyone is happening in the
camper, which is big, like life. I talk to it,
quietly, thank it, the light, the secret, held up
against the dark fields.

YOU MUST LOVE THIS

Love it all, man. Love your sorrow, love your sadness. Love
    your anger, hatred,
sorrow, again. Love it. Love it all, man.

Love the planets that spin their storms through your
    cosmic battlements, the storms of becoming, the
    storms of being, the storms of end. Love the storms.

Love the things that you have forgotten. All the days your
    children ran up to you and said things and gave you
    things and looked certain ways and now you can't
    remember shit, hardly, maybe one tone of voice or
    image of a face and now they aren't like that anymore,
    it is gone. Love that your wife has a way better
    memory than you. Love it. Love forget. Love gone.
    Love change, man. Love change.

Love the smelly Chinatown fish gut sidewalks. Love them.

Love the people that look at you like you don't belong.
    Love the idea that you don't belong. Love the idea of
    belong. Love the guy who made that up.

Love the Macy Street Liquor store and its winos, shades
    made of true western dust.

Love the prisoners in the sheriff's bus, who knows what
they might have done or not. Love them.
Love the sheriff, too, even though he is the slave ship
master of the unjust status quo and lost his cosmic
cable TV connection to the universe of love for a solid
middle class income, a house and boat and TiVo and
that is his problem, but love him.

Love Che Guevara, and all the T-shirts he lives on. Love
that he killed people. That he loved while he killed
and he did it to free the humble, the true, from their
humiliation at the hands of the criminal ruling class
and that one of the people he killed was some weird
special ed. kid's grandpa and the kid's mom got mad at
you for having a Che poster in your classroom and you
thought maybe Bob Marley's a better poster to have on
the wall cause he didn't kill anyone, but he smoked a
lot of weed. Love the confusion of truth and desire and
action.

Love the people fighting at the next table. Love when
you are the people fighting at the next table. Love
fighting. That we must fight. That we feel like shit
enough to pass it around. Love it. Love that it all boils
up and out of us and across the table and street and
into our bellies and veins or muscles, the fighting shit,
the anger, the piss, the unhappy with this shit and the
fucking fuck you, the fight and I don't know why. Love
it.

Love the anger in your children.
Love the anger in your wife.
Love the anger in your own hands, heart, belly, throat,
    eyes, and ears.
Love the anger in everything.
Love the spiritual blindness in everything.
Love the Spiritual Spiderman Lucha Libre masks on
    Olvera Street, that they are the beautiful masks of the
    mind, fighting clowns of the mind,
searching for the true fight of love. Love their blind desire.
Love the Spanglish spoken here. The Spanglish of the mind.
Love the city that has been lost to us forever. The city of
    the mind.
Love the societies and cultures that lay beneath our streets.
    The streets of the mind.
Love that they have been lost. Love that things will never
    be like they were.
Love that there are layers and layers of streets that will lay
    over us. All of us.
All of us of the mind.

Love the jasmine that blooms.
Love the tourist and his bus.
Love the hustler bum asking you for dollars, getting mad
    cause you said no. Love No. Love that there is a No, a
    Universal No. The Not. Love Not. That it is there. The
    other door of the mind, you can't have it.

Love the murder. Love the suicide.
Love what you cannot love.

Love that you cannot love it.
Love the impossibility of the task of love.
Love the impossible mission of our nature.
Love our imperial failure.
Love all our broken gods.
Love the mystery and the shower of light.
Love the darkness we spin in our minds.
Love our pointless defiance against, self, God, and nature.
Love Homework.
Love your plate and all that it holds.
Love your rage.
Love your repetition. Love that there is really only one or
    two things to say, but you keep thinking there are more
    and you keep saying them, but they are really only the
    same one or two things you already said.
Love your embarrassment.
Love your insanity, that you threw a kid's ice cream cone at
    work today. Who cares why? You did it. Love it.
Love how you disappoint your wife and children with
    your juvenile displays of inappropriate and irrational
    emotion, rage, throwing an ice cream cone, fighting
    teen obesity and diabetes in Hispanic Ghetto youth
    culture. Love the Hispanic ghetto youth culture and
    their 7 a.m. McDonald's ice cream smart asses saying
    "It's better than nothing." Love the Hispanic ghetto
    youth culture in your own mind that wants to eat tasty
    shit all day long and flip off the white dude teacher
    man, hey mister. Love it, them, all the thems, within
    you and without you.

Love how frightened you are by them, the ghetto culture
of violence and poverty, any ghetto, all ghettos, all is a
ghetto, prefab heads of state nuclear ghetto violence
and poverty of heart and mind, the youth culture
of extroverted soulless desperation, soul crying
desperation, with no power other than the power to
hurt themselves and they know it. Love it.

Love the frightened poor, the frightened poor within
you, the frightened poor that believe in possession as
security and the shallow powers of lust and rage.
Love them.

Love your own love of lust and rage.

Love the fist that wails fire, sun, at the sun, at the pain,
in pain. The lost demon protector against demons it
cannot fight. Love the walls it hits and builds at the
same time. Love the fire it fights with fire, burning
everything. Love the face and bones it makes and the
ones is destroys. Oh love them, love it, lost hand of fire.
Fucking sad lost hand of fire. Love it.

Love remorse, your remorse at being a fuck up, a fucked
up parent, husband, you're trying now, but you fucked
up. Love it. Love the fuck up. Love the guilt and shame.
Love knowing it was your fault, your problem, your
own broken house of bitter windows, your own toxic
mind shafts, love them, your own dirt lots of sad
dogs and rape that you refused to escape because you

were sure that there was gold, oil, a couple of bucks,
a shiny something, something in that dirt lot car lot
weed patch hundred million-year-old personal family
dinosaur junkyard of try and love, but you don't know
how, but that is how.

Love your rape. Love that they hurt you—the big they,
all of them, big hands of the faceless nobody, thus
everybody—left lane, super market, schoolyard,
grandpa, grandma, mom and dad, uncle, too, all of
them fucking hurt you. Love your hurt. Love hurt.
Love it. Love that shit freaking hurts, that this body is
all about hurt, that it gets hurt, body mind belly love
hurt the very thing you love.
Love your own brutal humiliation at the hands of your
protectors beneath a sun that would not shade
you from them, that would not shade them from
themselves. Love too bad. Love the one that hurt you.
Love that man. Those boys. It's all you can do. Love
that it is not possible. Can't happen. Love that, too.

Love your own soul's degradation at the hands of your
broken incarnations, murderer of innocents, violations
of the heart, the ravings of the empty fire trying to
build his light by blinding the sun. It can't happen.

Love the sun and its unforgiving heat.
Love the sun that does not shade but burns us to our own
purpose pure and full of bones made of water and
water turned to breath and empty light.

Love the holy empty, the bones, the darkness, the water,
   the house that time has built for your underwater
   schooling.

Love them.

Love the water that surrounds you.
Love the unskillful anger that erupts like molten flowers
   from this pool of hurt.
Love its fingers craving sunlight, water, pure now,
   salvation, craving to stop the wings of pain helicopters
   beating the brush of the mind, looking for snipers.
Love them, the snipers.

Love those who have left you.
Love those who have died.
Love that your parents left you, that they died, took their
   lives and fucked you up, love that they were so broken
   they couldn't fit into this skin and bones and drive the
   car to work and love you and themselves at the same
   time.
Love that they have left you.
That they abandoned you. That it wasn't your fault.
   That they did it and couldn't not do it. That that is
   the way it goes, the way it went and there is nothing
   that anyone can do about it, that's it, there is nothing
   anyone could have done about it, not you, not them,
   not me, not nobody, mister. Love abandoned. Love left.
   Love gone. Love leave, that things leave, that they

don't stick around, that they can't, that they need to
but don't. Love that we are things that come and go,
that get here and leave, that this is all there is to it.
Love it.

Love death. Love that we die and end and yes, though we
are spirit mostly, yes, we will never wear these clothes
again, and learn these things that we learn here, we
will never be here, right here, again, in this mouth
of time and body, being swallowed by the handsome
clothes of this life, right now. Love right now, that this
is the only this we know, the only this we can start
from. Love never again. Love the one and only. Love
the one and only and over and done, and done poorly,
yes, perhaps, but this is the only one of these, the only
name like this, these letters, this language, this face,
that I'm ever gonna see.

Love everything that is and isn't, should and shouldn't,
love sucks and doesn't.
Love what you can and what you cannot love.

Love the haters, love those who love hate, who hate you,
love what you hate, love that you hate. Love hate. Love
its broken winged pride sputtering toxic gasoline
falling angel tattered sail in the end of time ocean,
trying so hard to be right, to be right, to be right,
knowing that it can never be right, is never right, is
always wrong, oh sorrow of hatred, forever doomed,
fated, menacing power of world and mind, power of

steel sky or concrete river, power fueled by unseen
sorrow and fear, power needing to fill what cannot
be filled, sorrow that horror, fear, gnashing teeth
and screaming rivers of mind cannot be calmed by
gnashing and screaming heaven, so sad the wrong
heaven of hatred, the non-heaven of hatred.

Love wrong. Love sad. Love that wrong sad heaven.

Love the heaven that is not in us.
Love the heaven that sits and waits.
Love the heaven that can't be had in this life.

Love the shit that falls from your asshole. Love that it falls
from your asshole. Love that you need to create waste
in order to survive. Love the inefficient and flawed
creation that you are.

Love that you love eating greasy chicken alone at Zankou
Chicken in Hollywood, without the wife and kids and
friends, with no one at all, just you and too much food,
love that you ordered too much food. Love that the
chicken you are eating used to be alive, that it was
slaughtered inhumane mechanized factory of chicken
death, love that you are eating inhumane chicken
death with garlic lard sauce and loving it, love that the
chicken along with a handful of other animal species
have supported this line of society going back 100,000
years or something and it just keeps getting worse for
them. Love that we kill so much just to keep the air-

conditioning on and the computer running.
Love our lost need. The garlic sauce. The hummus.

Love the commercial exchange of shitty goods for shitty
    purposes, love the mind fuck shitty purpose of blind
    greed need fuck that is never satisfied, love never
    satisfied.
Oh love it. Love it, cause it made us, built this very house,
    this wall, this street, robbed the bank, killed the native,
    made the slave, in us all.
Love the slave in us all. Love the beaten and exploited
    and used and the broken and unlived, petty, jealous
    and treacherous life in all of us, love the hurt that it
    comes from, the beaten soul that writhes up poison,
    the beaten soul that belongs to this life, this planet,
    this light, to all lights, seen and unseen, felt and unfelt.
    Love the poor mind that made these chains, that makes
    them, that won't take them off.

Love the shitty ads on Sunset Boulevard, American
    Apparel that blast pedophile porno images of lost
    chicks in the rec room of lost chick sick man fantasy
    land. Love the T-shirts they sell. Love the hand bag
    happy americana mythology of cheap pussy that we
    buy.

Love the people that are better than you, all of them, the
    millions of them.
Love that you cannot stand them.
Love the need to be better. Love worse. Love the absurd

power of jealousy.

Love the poison of hierarchies. That you are addicted to
the vertical scale, the pointless

Scale of ideas and desires, the idea that somehow being
good or bad or better or known and not known will
mean anything to anyone, to your eternal light bulb,
to your cosmic can of tomato sauce, to the billions of
galaxies floating in your eyeball. Who cares? Love who
cares.

Love the teenage boys that walk tough-ass, laughing at
your middle-aged softness. Love softness, love being
fragile, love being so delicate the wind of passing cars
hurts you, the rustle of city planted tree frightens you,
love your softness, your not belonging in the hard
world of hurt and harm. Love your anger that arises
from this, your misplaced flower box of life. Who put
me here and why? And why am I always so scared and
mad? And what do I want and need and what I am
after? Love the soft questions, the soft answers.

Love that you can't stop thinking about how much you
suck and how much it all sucks and how much you
love it and it doesn't matter cause it's all so fucking
beautiful and it sucks and it's gonna end and that's
beautiful.

Love that you can't come up with a better way to say it.

Love the bodies that you share. Love the trap of family and
commitment.

Love that your wife moans disgusted and starts to cry
frustrated and desperate when you move to kiss her,
trying to get with her at night in your husband and
wife bed. Love that sex is not easy, is frustrating, that
you want it for all the wrong reasons and she knows
it, but they are the only reasons you have. Love your
broken reasons.

Love that you are stuck in this love and so is she. Love
the genius of stuck. No choice. Love no choice. The
wisdom of the no-choice train. Love that this whole
life deal is a no-choice train. You must grow old and
learn the sorrow of the body. You must learn the joy
and sorrow of the body, of life and no life, of here and
not here. Love that you get to touch things, man, want
things. Love it. Love want. Love desire. Love hunger.
Love need. Love all these things that can't be filled
or stopped. Love the craving hands that shape your
dewy bones, that give your wanting clay its broken fire.
Love the fire that turns this muddy wheel.

Love the wisdom of the trap. Love that it is all a trap,
that it all tapers off into the fugitive jungles of
disappointment because you cannot do with a body
what the spirit desires and needs.

Love.

Love that your love, when all is said and done, will have
loved much and hard and soft and vast and huge and
small and plain and there and not there and things

that couldn't be but are and shouldn't be, but had to.
Love what you cannot love. Love what you cannot love.
Love can't. Love limit. Love stop. Love edge, end, over.
Love the river that loses your name and that's it, into
a million other ended names, an ocean of ended names.
Love this limited mind and the rest of the universe that
just doesn't think like that, love it, man. Love it. Love
what you cannot love, just love it. That's all you can do.

3 A.M. IN MEXICO, 1996

I cannot sleep when there is this
smell of bonfires burning,
and the overwrought male voice of a
heartbroken singer coming from some stereo.

I cannot sleep when the Catholic spires are trapped
in a darkness they cannot deny, do not.
Blue neon crosses touch the stars.

Cars bump down the street.
Cathy sleeps, Penelope with
teething fever, sleeps
restless, a train yells.
Does a bird scream, surely, somewhere?
Johnny Future talks in his sleep
in my head. Will I ever like him?
My wife sleeps, sleepily, sighs, tries
to keep sleep asleep, tries.

I wonder: is this the beginning
of my adult life, right now, thinking
about masturbating, watching Mexican
MTV, waiting for a Beck video beside
the stars, and old men with microphones.

A man walks down a wet sidewalk.

The thin streets, walls hunching in,
bending everything towards a light,
then an open door, where people
eat tacos and drink cokes
and then the street
moves on, carrying a girl,
just a kid, across the cobbles
and up the stairs, to somewhere.
I couldn't tell you where,
cause I don't know.

A siren chirps.
I am awake and the world is somewhere.
The walls are blue.
There are airplanes in the sky somewhere
too, with the world.
I believe in sunrise.
I believe in my dreams.
I want to say this is beautiful,
but I am too tired to say that, really,
and the train will wake the baby,
I'm afraid.

I don't know how to end this thing.
I didn't even know I had started.

War is on T.V.
War makes bricks.
Bricks make walls
and that is what I

am really saying.

I cannot sleep when the revelers are loud,
walking drunk, ass grabbing, dog barking,
giggles down the sparkly street.

Good night, say the bombs of love.
Good night, say the birds of crime.
Good night, say the fires of dreams
unlived in the forest of my mind.

Good night, Good night
says the sunrise.

ABOUT THE AUTHOR

Steve Abee was born in Santa Monica, California and began writing after high school when he held a job as an orderly at St. John's Hospital. His mind started to unfold itself and he thought if he was going to save it he better start writing things down. "I saw the fragility and blessedness of lives and started to come apart in the wonderment of it all."

He is the author of the new novel *Johnny Future* with MacAdam/Cage; the underground sensation *The Bus: Cosmic Ejaculations of the Daily Mind in Transit* (Phony Lid Books), and the collection of short stories and poems *King Planet* (Incommunicado).

He lives and teaches in Los Angeles.

OTHER GREAT WRITE BLOODY BOOKS

THE GOOD THINGS ABOUT AMERICA
An illustrated, un-cynical look at our American Landscape. Various authors.
Edited by Kevin Staniec and Derrick Brown

JUNKYARD GHOST REVIVAL
with Andrea Gibson, Buddy Wakefield, Anis Mojgani, Derrick Brown, Robbie Q,
Sonya Renee and Cristin O'keefe Aptowicz

THE LAST AMERICAN VALENTINE:
ILLUSTRATED POEMS TO SEDUCE AND DESTROY
24 authors, 12 illustrators team up for a collection of non-sappy love poetry
Edited by Derrick Brown

SOLOMON SPARROWS ELECTRIC WHALE REVIVAL
Poetry Compilation by Buddy Wakefield, Anis Mojgani, Derrick Brown, Dan
Leamen & Mike McGee

STEVE ABEE, GREAT BALLS OF FLOWERS (2009)
New Poems by Steve Abee

SCANDALABRA
New poetry compilation by Derrick Brown

I LOVE YOU IS BACK
Poetry compilation (2004-2006) by Derrick Brown

BORN IN THE YEAR OF THE BUTTERFLY KNIFE
Poetry anthology, 1994-2004 by Derrick Brown

DON'T SMELL THE FLOSS
New Short Fiction Pieces by Matty Byloos

THE CONSTANT VELOCITY OF TRAINS
New Poetry by Lea Deschenes

HEAVY LEAD BIRDSONG
New Poems by Ryler Dustin

UNCONTROLLED EXPERIMENTS IN FREEDOM
New Poems by Brian Ellis

LETTING MYSELF GO
Bizarre God Comedy & Wild Prose by Buzzy Enniss

CITY OF INSOMNIA
New Poetry by Victor D. Infante

WHAT IT IS, WHAT IT IS
Graphic Art Prose Concept book by Maust of Cold War Kids and author Paul Maziar

IN SEARCH OF MIDNIGHT: THE MIKE MCGEE HANDBOOK OF AWESOME
New Poems by Mike McGee

ANIMAL BALLISTICS
New Poetry compilation by Sarah Morgan

NO MORE POEMS ABOUT THE MOON
NON-Moon Poems by Michael Roberts

CAST YOUR EYES LIKE RIVERSTONES INTO THE EXQUISITE DARK
New Poems by Danny Sherrard

LIVE FOR A LIVING
New Poetry compilation by Buddy Wakefield

SOME THEY CAN'T CONTAIN
Classic Poetry compilation by Buddy Wakefield

COCK FIGHTERS, BULL RIDERS, AND OTHER SONS OF BITCHES (2009)
An experimental photographic odyssey by M. Wignall

THE WRONG MAN (2009)
Graphic Novel by Brandon Lyon & Derrick Brown

YOU BELONG EVERYWHERE (2009)
A memoir and how to guide for travelling artists by Derrick Brown with Joel Chmara, Buddy Wakefield, Marc Smith, Andrea Gibson, Sonya Renee, Anis Mojgani, Taylor Mali, Mike McGee & more.

WWW.WRITEBLOODY.COM

WRITEBLOODY
QUALITY AMERICAN BOOKS

PULL YOUR BOOKS UP BY THEIR BOOTSTRAPS

Write Bloody Publishing distributes and promotes great books of fiction, poetry and art every year. We are an independent press dedicated to quality literature and book design, with offices in LA and Nashville, TN.

Our employees are authors and artists so we call ourselves a family. Our design team comes from all over America: modern painters, photographers and rock album designers create book covers we're proud to be judged by.

We publish and promote 8-12 tour-savvy authors per year. We are grass-roots, D.I.Y., bootstrap believers. Pull up a good book and join the family. Support independent authors, artists and presses.

Visit us online:

writebloody.com

Printed in the United States
150695LV00001B/5/P